DAVID CLARK

THE GLOBAL FINANCIAL CRISIS AND AUSTERITY

A basic introduction

POLICY PRESS INSIGHTS

First published in Great Britain in 2016 by

Policy Press
University of Bristol
1-9 Old Park Hill
Bristol
BS2 8BB
UK
t: +44 (0)117 954 5940
pp-info@bristol.ac.uk
www.policypress.co.uk

North America office:
Policy Press
c/o The University of Chicago Press
1427 East 60th Street
Chicago, IL 60637, USA
t: +1 773 702 7700
f: +1 773 702 9756
sales@press.uchicago.edu
www.press.uchicago.edu

© Policy Press 2016

British Library Cataloguing in Publication Data
A catalogue record for this book is available from the British Library.

Library of Congress Cataloging-in-Publication Data
A catalog record for this book has been requested.

ISBN 978-1-4473-3039-4 (paperback)
ISBN 978-1-4473-3040-0 (ePub)
ISBN 978-1-4473-3041-7 (Mobi)

The rights of David Clark to be identified as the author of this work has been asserted by him in accordance with the Copyright, Designs and Patents Act 1988.

The statements and opinions contained within this publication are solely those of the author and not of the University of Bristol or Policy Press. The University of Bristol and Policy Press disclaim responsibility for any injury to persons or property resulting from any material published in this publication.

Policy Press works to counter discrimination on grounds of gender, race, disability, age and sexuality.

Cover design by Andrew Corbett
Front cover: image kindly supplied by Getty
Printed and bound in Great Britain by CMP, Poole
Policy Press uses environmentally responsible print partners

To the memory of my parents, Albert and Phyllis,
no strangers to austerity

Contents

About the author

Now retired, David Clark was formerly head of social, community and political studies at Southampton Solent University. He taught public policy and management in a number of UK universities before working on a consultancy basis for several years, undertaking assignments for public sector clients in the fields of urban and rural regeneration, public health, and housing and land use planning. He has written widely on themes relating to administrative justice, urban and rural regeneration and public service reform in the UK, France and Canada, most recently in association with the Québec National School of Public Administration.

Acknowledgements

This book began life as a retirement project, and I am grateful to former colleagues in a number of universities for the intellectual stimulus they have provided over the years. I am particularly indebted to Brian Bowen, Ian Broad, Jim Doyle and Derek Williams, friends and former colleagues at what is now Southampton Solent University, for encouraging me to convert my various thoughts and jottings about the financial crisis into book form. I owe Derek a special debt of gratitude for reading and commenting on the whole draft.

I want to thank my cycling buddies, especially Terry Hammond and Mervyn Rowlinson, for lively conversation while pedalling the highways and byways of southern England (and sometimes farther afield), occasions during which we have often managed to put the banks, the British economy and the world in general to rights.

I am grateful to Emily Watt at Policy Press for her interest in this project, and to her colleagues Victoria Pittman, Laura Vickers and Laura Greaves, for their help and support in progressing it through to publication. I am no less grateful to Policy Press's two anonymous referees for their helpful comments on my initial draft, and their constructive advice on how to improve it.

My thanks also to Ken Blakemore for some sound advice.

My family has been a constant source of encouragement, as has my local support network of friends and neighbours. I am especially grateful to my wife Carol, who has lived with this project as much as I have. She has been a wise counsellor, an occasional critic and de facto project manager. Without her this book would not have been written.

Preface

Given the enormous impact of the 2008 financial crash and post-crash austerity on so many people's lives, several years on and it is hardly surprising that a veritable torrent of books has poured forth on this subject – mostly written by academics and journalists, but there have also been some by politicians, (former) regulators and market traders who were close to the action.

Interestingly, and disturbingly, many of the people who might have been expected to see the crisis coming – professional economists and financial and business journalists, for the most part – were caught unawares by it, more or less disqualifying themselves as credible commentators thereafter. To be fair, some prominent US-based economists did go public on their concerns about the housing bubble and the dangerous levels of risk building up in the financial system, but their warnings were dismissed by the true believers in the Panglossian orthodoxy (also known as the 'efficient markets hypothesis') that all was well with the financial markets, in the best of all possible worlds – that is, the Anglo-American world of free markets and light-touch regulation (Krugman, 2009).

In fact, there were quite a few Cassandras – economists and at least one US watchdog (regulator) – who saw some sort of financial crisis coming, but no one in a position of power and authority, whether politicians, central bankers or within the economics profession itself, wanted to listen to them (Galbraith, 2009). The watchdog who barked was Brooksley Born, chair of the Commodity Futures Trading

Commission from 1996 to 1999, whose warnings about the dangers posed by the huge and growing market in unregulated financial derivatives went unheeded by the Clinton administration and were disavowed by fellow-regulators.

Yes, it's a crowded market, but I do believe that there is room for an addition to the literature that is reasonably short and designed as an *entry-level* guide to the global financial crisis and its consequences.

Let me elaborate a little on the spirit in which I have written this book. As a retired university teacher, I want to retain the scholarly virtues of rigorous analysis, critical reflection and proper referencing of other people's work. I also want to avoid the characteristic academic vice of writing in a kind of vernacular or 'private language' that makes what is being written inaccessible to outsiders. And because the book straddles the disciplinary boundaries of finance, economics and politics/political science (my own specialism), I have made every effort to write it in plain English to make it accessible to as wide a range of people as possible from within the academic community, as well as to the serious general reader with little or no knowledge of these academic disciplines.

What is most disturbing about the Panglossian mindset (and it's easy for me to say this as I'm not a trained economist) is not that so few economists – and I think we can include regulators and financiers in this category as well – failed to predict the 2008 crash (the timing and precise contours of which were unknowable), but that the professional consensus was that such a crash was inconceivable. More precisely, that it was inconceivable that rational and efficient financial markets could implode from within, which is what happened in 2007-08, rather than as a result of some external shock.

This book is not going to systematically examine the efficient markets hypothesis alluded to above – or, for that matter, the alternative approaches and schools of thought that were pushed off the economics curriculum in many universities during the era of free market fundamentalism. Rather, its purpose is to help readers understand the origins and consequences of the great financial crash, and this means placing it in its historical and ideological context. What the book will do is illustrate the way in which the professional consensus among economists and economic policy-makers has changed over time, as well as outline the various policy responses of Western governments to the crash and ensuing recession. I have worked hard too, as a non-specialist in the field, to demystify the shadowy world of global finance, and to explain as clearly as I can how it spiralled out of control during the boom years preceding the crash.

The book also addresses a number of themes that economists tend to neglect, not least why the financial system that got us into the mess we're in is still, in many respects, unchanged from what it was like on the eve of the crash; and why one of the leading G7 (Group of Seven) advanced economies that meet annually to discuss matters of common interest – Canada – was more or less immune from the banking crisis. To shed light on matters such as these, we need to turn to *political economy* or a perspective on banking, finance and economics that takes into account the operation of politics, power and the contest of ideas.

Political economy? Well, at its most straightforward, the term refers to the intersection of economics and politics. 'Political economy' has been defined as a branch of the social sciences that studies the relationships between the market economy and the state (a nation or territory organised as a political community, under the rule of a government with the authority to raise taxes and operate an army and police force), using a diverse set of tools and methods drawn largely from economics, political science and sociology (see www. britannica.com). 'Political economy' is in fact the original name given to the academic discipline now known as 'economics', the change of name signifying the desire of the discipline to become a pure science, shorn of political and ethical dimensions that involve subjective value judgements (Chang, 2014, p 120).

Another, perhaps more useful way of understanding political economy is to think in terms of the 'supporting institutions' such as the rule of law, political stability, a sound currency and consumer and environmental protection that underpin properly functioning economic activity, and that are generally seen as the responsibility of governments or states to provide. This is not to say that policies imposed by governments or regulators are always effective. As John Kay demonstrates in the context of the much admired system of German vocational training, training policy works because, and only because, it is part of a subtle relationship between private and social institutions and the power and resources of the state that is not easily replicated elsewhere (Kay, 2004, p 341). If we are to understand the great financial crash and post-crash austerity, it is imperative that we probe the nature and effectiveness of the relationship between governmental and financial institutions. This is at the heart of a political economy approach.

David Clark

October 2015

Introduction

The so-called Great Recession of 2009, the biggest economic downturn since the Great Depression of the 1930s,[1] was a global economic recession sparked by the US sub-prime mortgage crisis and the subsequent credit crunch and financial crash of 2007-08. Years on and its effects, in the form of austerity, high levels of unemployment and of household and government debt,[2] and limited prospects for growth, have a continuing influence in many countries. 'Austerity' has been described as 'a form of voluntary deflation in which the economy adjusts through the reduction of wages, prices and public spending to restore competitiveness, which is (supposedly) best achieved by cutting the state's budget, debts and deficits' (Blyth, 2013, p 2).

The first chapter of this book describes how the contemporary banking and financial system works, and highlights the key role it has come to play in developed economies. Chapter Two tells the story of how, when a US housing bubble burst, trillions of dollars' worth of risky mortgages came to infect global markets, nearly bringing down some of the most strategically important financial institutions on the planet, as well as plunging most developed Western economies into recession. Together, these chapters should help readers gain a basic understanding of why the financial system imploded as it did in 2007-08, and how what started as a financial crisis became a broader economic and sovereign debt crisis.

Depending on how much you already know about the world of banking and finance, or indeed want to know about it, I anticipate that you may want to dip into the Appendix for more information on the various financial instruments, processes and institutions that are referred to in Chapters One and Two, either on a 'need to know' basis or perhaps more extensively. The A–Z rough guide provides considerably more extended commentary than you would normally find in a conventional glossary or jargon buster on the constituent parts of the global financial system and the innovative financial products that are heavily implicated in the crisis, and it should give you a better technical understanding of the workings of global finance. But it may also overload you and disrupt the flow of your reading, so it may be a good idea to read through Chapters One and Two fairly quickly, without consulting the Appendix, with a view to getting the gist of what is being written. Think of the A–Z guide more as a semi-detached 'primer' that you can return to as and when you wish in order to extend your knowledge of banking and finance.

The entries in the rough guide will be highlighted in bold type when first encountered in the text. One or two do not appear until later in the book, and these will also be highlighted in bold when first introduced. In fact, you've come across three of the entries already – derivatives, (asset) bubble and government or 'sovereign' debt (and there's a fourth, monetary policy, in the notes at the end of this Introduction) – but you'll meet them again shortly in Chapters One or Two, where they'll be in bold type. There's one more entry to come in this Introduction, this time in bold type as you won't come across it again. You may wish to check it out in the A–Z guide in a moment.

Yes, this is complex stuff and it will require application and some perseverance on your part, but it's not rocket science. That said, there is a sense in which Wall Street, the City of London and some other hubs of the global financial system do resemble a 'rocket experiment gone wrong': rocket scientists did indeed help to make the financial crisis happen (Smith, 2009). These are the financial engineers or 'quants': mathematicians and physicists recruited from leading universities to design the financial products and computer algorithms (see **algorithmic trading**) that led traders to take on ever greater risk in the search for new markets and new profits.

Most people, myself included until embarking on this project, see finance and the financial sector as arcane and mysterious. This serves the interests of bankers and financiers, whose power and perceived expertise is reinforced every time a term such as 'complex derivatives' is used in the popular media (Scott, 2013, p 29). One of the main aims of this short book is to encourage you to embrace the idea that the functioning, and malfunctioning, of the global financial system is not really, in its essentials, quite so complex and impenetrable as it seems. You really don't need to be a rocket scientist to gain a basic understanding of why a global, interconnected network of financial institutions and markets imploded in the near-meltdown of 2008; or why, due to a misplaced belief in the self-regulating, self-correcting nature of financial markets, the participants in the system behaved as they did in the boom years running up to the crash.

I, too, feel moral outrage at the greed of bankers, but I do not believe that the ethics of market participants, however fraudulent or predatory their behaviour, is the real cause of the financial crash. Nor do I believe that 'to examine the causes, domestic and global, of the current financial and economic crisis', which is what the National Commission established by Congress in 2009 was mandated to do in respect of the US (Financial Crisis Inquiry Commission, 2011), will tell you everything that you need to know about what has been described by Ben Bernanke, chair of the Federal Reserve (the US central bank – see Chapter One) from 2006 to 2014, as the 'worst financial crisis in global history, including the Great Depression' (see Financial Crisis Inquiry Commission, 2011, p xxii). This is because, although it is undoubtedly an 'outlier' in terms of its scale and impact on the real economy, there are plenty of parallels between the 2008 crisis and previous crises in the history of modern capitalism.[3] What the deregulation of financial markets in the 1980s and 1990s certainly did do, however, was to enlarge the opportunities for being greedier than had ever been realistically possible before (Kynaston, 2012, p ix).

To really make sense of the global financial crisis, in other words, we need to take a more expansive view, and position it as the latest in a long line of booms, bubbles and busts that have punctuated the history of capitalism as far back as the 1637 tulip mania in Holland, when the price of rare tulip bulbs soared to absurd heights and then crashed. Above all, we need to reflect on why it is that capitalist economies are so crisis-prone. Actually, what I've just written is a bit too simplistic. First, because capitalism in its recognisably modern form of industrial capitalism dates only from the last third of the 18th century; and second, because we need to distinguish between crises *in* capitalism (regular cycles of booms and busts) and crises *of* capitalism (spectacular financial crashes and periods of instability that lead to far-reaching economic, social and political change) (see Gamble, 2009, p 7).

This theme – that in the history of modern capitalism crises are the norm, not the exception (Roubini and Mihm, 2011) – is explored more fully in Chapter Three. There the focus shifts away from banking and finance to political economy, and you will be introduced to a rather different subject matter, including one particular perspective on the crisis – the 'regulation approach' – that rarely sees the light of day outside certain parts of the academy and can, alas, be equally impenetrable to the non-specialist. Chapter Four consists of two mini-case studies of real-world variation in the operation of finance-led capitalism in North America and the UK. The first explores the return of the super-rich and the second Canada's seeming immunity from the crisis. Chapter Five surveys the various policy responses to the great financial crash of governments in the US, the UK and continental Europe. Austerity and deficit reduction policies have been applied with great vigour and with damaging political consequences in the Eurozone,[4] and there is a particular focus in this chapter on the ongoing Greek debt crisis. The final chapter, Chapter Six, considers the nature of the post-recession recovery now under way, takes stock of current banking reform, and asks whether the crisis is really over.

Notes

[1] A 'recession' is officially defined as a period of at least six months during which gross domestic product (GDP) (the total monetary value of what has been produced within a country over a given period of time) contracts, as opposed to a 'depression', which is the period of time before the real level of GDP regains its previous high. The Great Depression was a worldwide depression, the longest and deepest of the 20th century, that began with a catastrophic collapse of share prices on the New York Stock Exchange in October 1929 and lasted in most countries until the late 1930s. It had devastating effects on rich and poor nations alike. Unemployment in the US rose to 25 per cent and in some countries to a third or more of the workforce. International trade fell by more than 50 per cent (Wikipedia). For a clear, succinct account of four 'candidate' explanations for what caused the Great Depression, see Bootle (2012, pp 32-40).

[2] Government debt is the total amount of money owed by a national government to its creditors. In the US and other federal states government debt may also refer to the debt of a provincial, state or municipal government. By contrast, the *annual deficit* refers to the difference between government tax receipts and spending in a single year, that is, the increase (or decrease) of debt over a particular year.

[3] Capitalism, as we understand the term today, is an economic system in which a country's trade, industry and means of production such as land and factories are, for the most part, in the hands of private owners and operated for profit in competitive markets. In the rich, developed countries of the world, such economies operate within a framework of democratic politics, and it is important to be aware that there are a number of national and regional varieties of 'democratic capitalism' or 'capitalist democracy' – 'that (political) formation which tries to unite an economy based on principles of market allocation and private property (capitalism) with a political system based on popular competition for political influence and leadership (democracy)' (Moran, 2009, p xiii) – to be found across the globe. This variety is mapped out in Chapter Four.

[4] The Eurozone, officially the euro area, is an economic and monetary union of 19 European Union (EU) member states that have adopted the euro (€) as their common currency and sole legal tender. The Eurozone consists of Austria, Belgium, Cyprus, Estonia, Finland, France, Germany, Greece, Ireland, Italy, Latvia, Lithuania, Luxembourg, Malta, the Netherlands, Portugal, Slovakia, Slovenia and Spain (Wikipedia). Within the Eurozone, monetary policy is the responsibility of the European Central Bank but the EU does not have tax and spending (fiscal) powers of its own. Fiscal policy

is controlled, ostensibly at least, by individual member states. As we will see in Chapter Five, this no longer really applies to members of the EU who have ratified the 'fiscal compact'. This includes all EU member states other than the UK, the Czech Republic and Croatia.

ONE

Banking and shadow banking: an overview

Banks are a structural equivalent of hostage takers: if you want to save the life of the hostage, you had better do what banks request. (Offe, 2015, p 17)

Why banks matter

If economists can be blamed for not anticipating the financial crash, then bankers (rightly) stand accused of causing it. A healthily functioning banking system performs a number of key economic functions, and four, arguably, are of particular importance. First, banks operate the payments system without which most financial transactions could not occur. Second, they take in customers' deposits, thereby encouraging saving. Third, they channel funds from individual savers to small and medium-sized enterprises, and in so doing finance business investment. And fourth, they make mortgage and other personal loans, enabling families to purchase homes and consumer goods, activities which in turn support economic growth. Sometimes banks fail to perform these functions satisfactorily and go bust. This is normally because banks don't just create debt in the form of mortgages and loans, but take on debt themselves to make investments and acquire additional **assets**, and in doing so become *over-leveraged* ('leverage' refers to the practice of using borrowed money to purchase an asset). This, essentially, is how the US housing bubble that preceded the 2008 crash was created.

Let's briefly consider the 'charge sheet' against the banks before looking more closely at how the banking and financial system actually works. Four inter-linked charges can be brought against the banking system as it was operating at the beginning of the 21st century. The first is that some banks had become too big, both in absolute terms and relative to the size of national economies. The 2008 crash demonstrated that the very biggest banks could not be allowed to fail because if they did, many other businesses (including other banks), as well as households and employees, would go under too. National governments were effectively held hostage, having to step in and rescue 'their' banks at great cost to those countries' public finances.

The second charge is that the 'too big to fail' banks had (and continue to have) too strong an incentive to take on excessive risk, since governments will bail them out in an emergency. Realising that megabanks have an implicit government guarantee, the financial markets are willing to lend them money at lower interest rates than to smaller banks, which makes it harder for the smaller banks to compete and deters new entrants (see Johnson and Kwak, 2010, pp 204-5).

The third charge concerns the banks' usefulness to society. In 2009, in a round-table discussion organised by *Prospect* magazine, the former UK bank regulator (Lord) Adair Turner described some areas of banking – those involving the complex financial instruments to be revealed shortly – as 'socially useless'. More recently, citing data compiled by the economist Alan Taylor and his colleagues, Turner has written that:

> … with very few exceptions the banks' primary activity up to the 1920s and even the 1970s was non-mortgage lending to business but by 2007 banks in most countries had turned primarily into real estate lenders. The intermediation of household savings for productive investment in the business sector constitutes only a

very minor share of what modern banking systems do today. (Turner, 2015, p 26)

Linked to this is the charge that the high salaries on offer in banking and finance were driving the smartest graduates, like those 'quants' mentioned in the Introduction, away from other sectors of the economy where they would be more usefully employed.

The fourth charge is that banks had become too powerful, as evidenced in their ability to insulate themselves from effective regulation and even from criminal law enforcement (Ferguson, 2014). More generally, the allegation is that bankers, through their contributions to political parties and the 'revolving door' between the financial services industry and government, had come to enjoy excessive political as well as economic power – that they had, in other words, become a self-serving part of a cohesive 'financial-political elite' (Fazi, 2014, p 16). As used in the social sciences, the term 'elite' does not refer, as it does in everyday usage, to a small group of people who excel in some aspect of life, but to those who by virtue of occupying leadership positions in government and business organisations have a determining influence over the public policy agenda and policy outcomes. The Canadian political scientist James Meisel (1958) held that effective ruling elites possessed three Cs: group consciousness (a sense of unity); coherence (mutual recognition of commitments and interests separating them out from the non-elite); and conspiracy (meaning a common will to action rather than secret machinations).[1]

How banks work

Banks are often described as financial intermediaries that facilitate the channelling of funds between lenders and borrowers. In the traditional model, a bank takes in deposits from its customers (which are regarded as its liabilities because customers can ask for them back at any moment) and makes long-term loans (which are its assets) to individuals and businesses in the 'real' economy. Banks also hold buffers of what is known in banking parlance as **capital** and elsewhere as equity (see

stocks, shares and equity), which is the money their shareholders put in. If the loan goes bad, this capital serves as a shock absorber: it is the shareholder capital, not the deposits, that takes the hit.

In practice, banks do not wait for a customer to deposit money before they make a new loan to someone else. This is because most countries have institutionalised a system known as *fractional reserve banking*, which enables banks to hold only a small reserve of the funds deposited and lend out the rest for profit. It is only if more and more loans go bad and the capital gets exhausted that banks run into real trouble. For this reason, they are subject to minimum *capital adequacy requirements* based on an international set of capital standards known as the Basel Accords (see **Basel III**).

In fact, and contrary to a widespread misconception, banks are not so much intermediaries recycling savings into loans as active creators of money, **credit** and purchasing power in the economy, either through making loans, buying existing assets or when customers draw down on their overdrafts (Werner, 2012; Ryan-Collins et al, 2014; Turner, 2015). This is how Positive Money, a UK not-for-profit organisation committed to 'democratising' money and banking, explains how banks create money:

> … when a bank makes a loan, for example to someone taking out a mortgage to buy a house, it does not typically do so by giving them thousands of pounds worth of banknotes. Instead, it credits their bank account with a bank deposit of the size of the mortgage. At that moment, new money is created. For this reason, some economists have referred to bank deposits as "fountain pen money", created at the stroke of bankers' pens when they approve loans. (Positive Money, nd)

Substitute digital money or 'keystroked electronic entries on bank balance sheets' (Wray, 2015, p 41) for 'fountain pen money' and arguably we have a more apt description of contemporary money creation, but the essential idea – that when depositors spend their accounts are debited, and the accounts of recipients are credited –

remains the same. No less an authority than the Bank of England has endorsed the view that most of the money in the modern economy is created by banks making loans: 'whenever a bank makes a loan, it simultaneously creates a matching deposit in the borrower's bank account, thereby creating new money' (McLeay et al, 2014, p 1). This means that the creation of credit and purchasing power in the wider economy is largely determined by the choices made by banks as to which activities (lending to property developers, say, as opposed to lending to small businesses) get keystroked finance (Wray, 2015, p 47).

Retail banking is the visible face of banking to the general public, and refers to the division of a *commercial* bank (one whose main business is deposit taking and extending credit to borrowers in the form of loans) that deals directly with retail customers (individuals and smaller businesses) on the high street. The term *corporate* or *wholesale* banking is generally used to describe that aspect of banking that relates to larger businesses and corporations. Commercial and retail banks must ensure that they have enough money to repay their customers, so they need to own some safe assets that they can sell quickly (Coggan, 2009, p xii).

Investment banks, or the investment banking arms of commercial banks, 'underwrite' (guarantee the sale of) 'stock' and **bond** issues: these are types of **security** that represent an ownership position in a publicly-traded corporation (stock) or a creditor relationship with a governmental body or corporation (bond). Such banks also provide investment management services for large institutional investors such as **pension funds**, **mutual funds** and **hedge funds**; trade on their own account; and advise companies on market activities such as mergers and acquisitions. A typical investment bank will engage in some or all of the following activities:

- raise equity capital, helping to launch an 'initial public offering' (IPO) of shares, as with the partial sale of the Royal Mail to institutional investors and the UK public in 2013;
- raise debt capital (the capital that a business raises by taking out a loan), for example, issuing corporate bonds to help raise money for a factory expansion;

- launch new financial products such as **mortgage-backed securities (MBS)**;
- engage in *proprietary trading*, where teams of in-house traders are given free rein to speculate on stocks, bonds, currencies and commodities (oil, wheat and so on) using the bank's own money (its equity capital) – together with large amounts of borrowed money – as opposed to that of its depositors.

In addition, investment banks have been able to operate their own hedge funds.

As indicated above, some commercial banks also have investment divisions. Indeed, the distinction between the two sorts of bank has become much less meaningful since the onset of the financial crisis. On the eve of the great financial crash, there were five major free-standing Wall Street investment banks. A year later they had all either gone bust, been forced to merge with a commercial bank or been re-designated as bank-holding companies allowed to take customer deposits but subject to greater federal regulation. Investment banking still takes place, of course, but no longer in free-standing institutions. So, too, a ban on the practice of proprietary trading by Wall Street banks was imposed by US regulators in 2013 (see below).

Historically, there has been a social class dimension to the split between investment and commercial banks, and this still holds. Investment banks are 'rich people's banks and intermediaries' while commercial banks take the savings of ordinary people and turn them into loans (Mason, 2009, pp 61-2). In the 1950s US investment banks became known as 'white shoe banks' after the white buckskin loafers sported by the Ivy League graduates who were recruited to work in them.

The primary function of a *central bank* such as the Bank of England or the US Federal Reserve (the Fed) is to manage the nation's money supply (see **monetary policy**) through active duties such as managing interest rates, setting the *reserve requirement* (which obliges banks to hold some fraction of their deposits in cash or in deposits with the central bank), and acting as a lender of last resort to the banking sector during times of bank insolvency or financial crisis. Central banks usually also have supervisory powers, intended to prevent bank runs and to reduce the risk that commercial banks and other financial institutions engage in reckless or fraudulent behaviour. Central banks in most developed nations are institutionally designed to be independent of political interference, that is, interference from elected politicians.

The *reserve requirement* governs the proportion of its assets that a bank must hold in cash. This should not be confused with capital adequacy requirements that govern the ratio of a bank's capital (equity) to its assets. Banks use both borrowed (debt) and 'unborrowed' money (money the bank has received from its shareholders, along with retained profits) to make their loans and other investments. The capital (adequacy) requirement is the fraction of a bank's investment assets that must be funded with unborrowed money. Such capital regulation is put into place to ensure that banks do not take on excess debt or leverage and become insolvent. This is rather like a mortgage holder being required to make a down payment when buying a house.

Because unborrowed funds are obtained without any promise to make specific payments at particular times, having capital equity enhances the bank's ability to control or absorb losses on its investments. Capital regulation does not mean that banks are forced to hold cash that could otherwise be put to work in the real economy (Admati and Hellwig, 2013, p 6).

Financial globalisation and the shadow banking system

The massive (and disproportionate) growth of the financial sector originated in the 1980s as finance became increasingly deregulated, increasingly global in nature, increasingly de-linked from the real economy (the part of the economy that is concerned with producing goods and non-financial services) and increasingly opaque. In this new era, banks could raise money from the international **money markets**, refreshing their capital as needed in a seemingly unending supply of credit. The vast expansion of **securitisation** – a way of bundling up mortgages and other forms of debt such as credit card repayments into bonds that are then sold to investors – allowed banks to offload the long-term risk of these debts to others and so create a supply of new capital for re-investment. In the words of the Canadian economist Jim Stanford (2008), the tail soon came to wag the dog; these new securities became gigantic speculative markets of their own, worth far more than all the residential homes in the land.

Let's be clear about this: banks still made mortgage loans, but no longer with the intention of holding them through to maturity (the 'originate to hold' model) but with a view to selling them on, usually to an investment bank, which performed its financial wizardry on them and offered pieces of the resulting pool of mortgage bonds to eager buyers (investors) in what became known as the 'originate to distribute' model (Coggan, 2009, p 30; Smith, 2011, pp 10-11). The process of securitisation created *liquidity* (the ability to convert an asset into cash with little or no loss in value) by enabling investors to buy into a large pool of mortgages, and it enabled banks to engage in more lending than previously.

The 1980s were the beginning of the era, too, of the 'Great Moderation' or reduction in the volatility of business cycle fluctuations that enabled bankers, regulators, politicians and the media to celebrate the economic benefits that were perceived to flow from an innovative financial sector and its capacity to disperse risk more broadly across deregulated financial markets, where national governments no longer imposed controls on the free movement of capital. The intellectual roots of the Great Moderation lie within the mainstream economics profession's *theory of efficient and rational markets* – a theory that ascribes to financial markets a superior capacity (superior to regulators) to monitor, measure and anticipate risk (Froud et al, 2012). This theory, also known as the 'efficient markets hypothesis' – that assets traded on financial markets are always valued correctly because, if they were not, traders could profit by buying or selling overpriced assets, quickly eliminating any divergence from intrinsic values – is a core component of *neoliberalism*.

Also known as market fundamentalism (Kaletsky, 2010), neoliberalism signifies both a generalised belief (or *ideology*, denoting a system of beliefs which can be used both to justify existing social and political arrangements and also to mobilise people for action) that the state and its interventions are obstacles to economic and social development, and a corresponding set of policy prescriptions – such as the privatisation of state assets, liberalisation of trade and deregulation of financial and labour markets – for maximising the role of free markets. Ironically, it requires a 'strong' state to implement such free market policies (see Gamble, 1994).

Neoliberalism gathered momentum in the 1980s, most notably in the US and the UK, as a politically driven project to dismantle and replace the post-war Keynesian variant of capitalist democracy[2] following the inability of Keynesian policies to anticipate and deal with 'stagflation': a situation of low growth and high unemployment combined with high inflation. This happened during the 1970s, when world oil prices rose dramatically, fuelling sharp inflation in developed countries.

Much of the new lending and borrowing in the years of the Great Moderation occurred in the *shadow banking system*, a term for the collection of financial intermediaries involved in facilitating the creation of credit across the globe whose members are not subject to regulatory oversight in the manner of 'normal' (deposit-taking) banks. The system includes investment banks, hedge funds, **private equity** firms, the money markets, **monoline insurers**, and **conduits and special purpose vehicles (SPVs)** – separate legal entities that are involved in the process of converting a pool of 'illiquid' debt assets such as mortgage and credit card repayments into a more complex security where investors can 'pick and mix' the risks on offer.

The system is mostly unregulated, opaque and located in offshore (or onshore) tax havens, with the consequence that shadow banks are likely to be highly leveraged. In 2008, the most common (secret) jurisdictions for US securitisations were the Cayman Islands and the state of Delaware; for European securitisations, Ireland, Luxembourg, Jersey and the UK (see BIS, 2009; Shaxson, 2012).

In the run-up to the credit crunch, SPVs and conduits typically borrowed heavily in the short-term money and commercial paper (CP) markets (see **money market funds [MMFs], asset–backed**

commercial paper [ABCP][3] and **repurchase agreements [repos])**, to invest longer term in higher yielding mortgage-backed securities (MBS). However, much of the shadow banking system (temporarily) collapsed during the credit crunch and subsequent financial crash. The process of recycling short-term borrowed money to fund the issue of trillions of dollars' worth of tradeable securities fuelled a massive lending boom in the mid-2000s, with the issue of securitised products peaking at more than US$4.5 trillion in the third quarter of 2007 (Luttrell et al, 2012, Appendix B). Problems arose when the securities pledged as collateral for short-term borrowing had their ratings questioned and/or downgraded, and the rest of the participants in the system, who lend to and borrow from each other, began to require more interest in exchange for taking on higher risk. As asset prices began to fall globally, so investors were much less willing to buy or 'roll over' ABCP.

Trading in **derivatives** enables investors to invest in particular financial products or asset classes (and also to speculate on movements in various rates and indexes) without having to own them directly. A stock market *futures contract*, for example, allows investors to make bets on the value of a stock market index such as the FTSE 100 (an index of the hundred companies listed on the London Stock Exchange with the highest share valuation or 'market capitalisation') without having to buy or sell any shares. Greatly facilitated by the abolition of foreign exchange controls in Western countries (see Chapter Three), the scale of foreign exchange dealing increased from around US$70 billion a day in 1988 to US$3.2 trillion a day in 2007. At least half of these daily transactions involved buying currency derivatives not for the purpose of spending the currency in the country where it was legal tender, but to resell it, swap it or take a bet on its future price (Mason, 2009, p 65).

By the early 2000s banks were becoming increasingly 'levered up', making loans to other financial institutions that were not matched by deposits. Bank lending was used to finance investment in MBS and other derivatives because the returns and fee income were higher than could be obtained by lending to small and medium-sized enterprises or to the government, with the underwriters who packaged and sold **structured finance** products, the *credit rating agencies* such as Fitch, Moody's and Standard & Poor's (S&P) that gave their seal of approval, and the guarantors who wrote protection against default all collecting fees for their part in the securitisation process.

By 2008, there was a £900 billion gap between the money lent by UK banks and the money they had taken in from depositors. That £900 billion was all obtained on the money markets from other financial institutions, including other banks. In the event, much of that vast sum was demanded back in 2007 and 2008, as fears increased that banks across the world were facing losses and might not be able to repay their debts (Peston and Knight, 2012, p 41). In the US, the assets of the Wall Street investment bank Goldman Sachs quadrupled between 1999 and 2007, growing at a rate of 21 per cent a year: Bank of America's assets grew by 14 per cent, and Citigroup's by 12 per cent – growth made possible by raising debt to equity ratios from 17:1 to 32:1 in the case of Goldman Sachs, from 18:1 to 27:1 in the case of Bank of America, and from 18:1 to 32:1 in Citigroup's case (Panitch and Gindin, 2013, p 306).

Rapid financial globalisation has been accompanied by an increase in cross-border financial flows and by the growing interconnectedness of a relatively small number of what the **International Monetary Fund (IMF)** terms 'large, complex financial institutions' (LCFIs), and the **Financial Stability Board (FSB)** 'global systemically important banks' (G-SIBs) that are engaged, either directly or through affiliates in the shadow banking system, in banking, securities and insurance operations. As the main intermediaries at the centre of the global financial system, these LCFIs or G-SIBs actively raise and channel funds from investors (often other LCFIs) to borrowers (often other LCFIs) both within and across national borders. Total financial sector assets, as measured by the Bank for International Settlements (an international organisation of central banks), grew very rapidly in recent years, from US$13.2 trillion in 2002 to US$30.5 trillion in 2009 (IMF, 2010).

As we'll see in the next chapter, the realisation that these giant international banks were the main channel for transmitting the mortgage crisis in the US and the sovereign debt crisis in the Eurozone to other countries, prompted the FSB to begin publishing an annual list of G-SIBs in 2011. The following banks were included in the November 2014 list (compiled using end-2013 data), nine of them headquartered in the US, six in Asia and 15 in Europe (four in France, three in the UK, two each in Spain and Switzerland, and one each in Germany, Italy, Sweden and the Netherlands): Agricultural Bank of China, Bank of America, Bank of China, Bank of New York Mellon, Barclays, BBVA (Banco Bilbao Vizcaya Argentaria), BNP Paribas, Citigroup, Credit Suisse, Deutsche Bank, Goldman Sachs, Groupe BPCE (Banque Populaire Caisse d'Epargne), Group Crédit Agricole, HSBC, ING Bank, Industrial and Commercial Bank of China Limited, J.P. Morgan Chase, Mitsubishi UFJ FG, Mizuho FG, Morgan Stanley, Nordea, Royal Bank of Scotland, Santander, Société Générale, Standard Chartered, State Street, Sumitomo Mitsui FG, UBS, Unicredit Group, and Wells Fargo.[4] By virtue of its size, complexity and interconnectedness with other financial institutions, the failure of any one of these 30 banks would, in the FSB's judgement, cause significant disruption to the wider global economy – and for that reason these banks are subject to stricter capital adequacy requirements under Basel 111 than are other banks.

Notes

[1] The term 'elite' can also be used to denote the broader social and occupational grouping(s) from which the ruling elite is drawn, and whose interests the ruling elite defends and advances.

[2] Keynesianism refers to the various schools of thought based on the ideas of British economist John Maynard Keynes (1883-1946) that advocate a proactive role for the state in managing modern economies. Advocates of Keynesian economics argue that the operation of free markets can lead to inefficient macro-economic outcomes (those effecting economy-wide phenomena such as levels of employment, growth and prices) which require active policy responses by state institutions, particularly monetary policy actions by the central bank and fiscal policy ('tax and spend') actions by the government to stabilise output over the business cycle.

[3] ABCP programmes were created in the 1980s as a way of enabling banks to avoid capital adequacy regulations by moving seemingly safe short-term, secured debt off their balance sheets, with the money raised from the issue of ABCP being used to fund the purchase of more assets to securitise. ABCP risk is secured by the expected cash flows from the asset pools and by the underlying assets of the sponsoring bank, and investors have claim to those assets. A special purpose vehicle (SPV) can pay a fee to a third party to provide external credit enhancement (such as a guarantee by a monoline insurance company).

[4] One bank (Agricultural Bank of China) has been added to the list of G-SIBs published in 2013, increasing the overall number to 30. Three banks that were included in the 2011 list were removed in 2013 – Dexia (Belgium), Commerzbank (Germany) and Lloyds Banking Group (UK) – and three added: BBVA, Standard Chartered and Industrial and Commercial Bank of China Limited (see FSB, 2014).

TWO

From boom to bust
and beyond

When the music stops, in terms of liquidity, things will be complicated. But as long as the music is playing, you've got to get up and dance. We're still dancing. (Comments made by Charles 'Chuck' Prince, former chair and chief executive of Citigroup, in an interview with *The Financial Times* in Japan, 9 July 2007, quoted in Nakamoto and Wighton, 2007)

Sub-prime mortgages, the credit crunch and the great financial crash of 2008

The rise in mortgage lending in the US was the proximate cause of the 2007 credit crunch and subsequent financial crash of 2008. In a nutshell, speculative lending by US financial institutions, especially of mortgage-backed **collateralised debt obligations (CDOs)**, created a vast housing bubble (see **asset bubble**) in 2001-06. When banks were deregulated in the 1980s, mortgage markets stopped being essentially national institutions and entered a new era of international bond markets in which mortgage debt began to circulate around the globe. This allowed originating banks to bundle up mortgages into bonds (mortgage-backed securities [MBS] and CDOs) and to sell them on to institutional investors such as insurance companies and pension funds, looking for what they thought were long-term, secure assets. Unlike when they made loans to hold through to maturity, under this 'originate to distribute' approach, banks no longer risked making losses if the mortgage loan defaulted (Financial Crisis Inquiry Commission, 2011, p 89). This global circuit of mortgage debt fuelled the massive indebtedness of owner-occupiers in many Western countries in the 1990s and 2000s.

Numerous CDOs were guaranteed by monoline insurers who promised to reimburse investors for any losses on them, including the riskier tranches backed by sub-prime mortgages (loans granted to individuals with poor credit histories, who would not qualify for a conventional mortgage), in exchange for premium payments (see **credit default swaps [CDS]**). The percentage of sub-prime mortgages originated during a given year rose from about 8 per cent historically to approximately 20 per cent in the period from 2004 to 2006, with much higher percentages in some parts of the US. A large proportion of these sub-prime mortgages, over 90 per cent in 2006, were adjustable rate mortgages (ARMs), where the initial interest rate was fixed at a low level after which it was reset periodically, sometimes every month, at a variable, and often much higher rate (Wikipedia, Sub-prime mortgages).

Furthermore, US households had become increasingly indebted, with the ratio of debt to disposable income rising from 68 per cent in 1980 to a peak of 128 per cent at the end of 2007, much of this increase being mortgage-related (Wikipedia, Household debt). When house prices across the US declined steeply after peaking in mid-2006, it became more difficult for borrowers to refinance their loans, and as ARMs began to reset at higher interest rates, mortgage defaults soared. Securities backed with mortgages, including sub-prime mortgages – widely held by financial institutions globally – lost most of their value and became 'toxic assets'. Mortgage-backed bonds also had the unfortunate effect of removing the lines of communication between the mortgage borrower and the original lender. Suddenly, large investors controlled the collateral; as a result, negotiations over late mortgage payments were by-passed for the 'direct to **foreclosure**' model of an investor looking to cut his or her losses (Investopedia, The fuel that fed the sub-prime meltdown).

Defined as 'a severe shortage of money or credit', the credit crunch occurred because finance providers from outside the normal banking system – such as hedge funds, pension funds and insurance companies – turned off the tap in respect of certain kinds of credit. The crunch was precipitated by panic in the ABCP and 'repo' markets. As investors tried to figure out who was holding the toxic securitised assets, suspicion soon fell on the conduits and SPVs that were key players in the rush to securitisation.

This is because there is an intrinsic weakness in their mode of funding: they borrowed money by issuing short-term ABCP to finance the issue of long-dated securities whose assets included high-risk sub-prime loans. Money raised from the issues was then used to purchase more assets to securitise. In theory, conduits made a greater return on the issue of securitised assets than they paid out in interest on CP, but such funding schemes only work while the market has confidence in the value of the collateral backing the CP. When investors started to have qualms about CDOs and other *asset-backed securities* such as student loans and commercial loans and leases, the SPVs and sponsoring banks were squeezed in a vice: short-term funding disappeared and there was a collapse in the value of the assets they held.

Unable to renew their existing ABCP, these 'off-balance sheet' vehicles experienced a *liquidity crunch* in 2007 as other institutions stopped lending to them. In the space of a few weeks in the spring and summer of 2007, investors moved US$200 billion out of the ABCP market, and the SPVs and conduits faced much higher borrowing costs. Some creditors refused to lend money at any cost, forcing the banks to bring their SPV exposures back onto their balance sheets (Roubini and Mihm, 2011, p 93). The boom-turned-credit crunch culminated in the bankruptcy of one of the biggest, most leveraged players in this market, the Wall Street investment bank Lehman Brothers, in September 2008. The Bush administration's decision to let Lehman fail exposed the global banking system to the risk posed by 'unbacked' CDS, forcing central banks and governments across the world to intervene to bail out their banks and 'socialise' their losses – at an estimated cost to national taxpayers of between US$3 and US$13 trillion (Blyth, 2013, p 5).

Commentators such as Raghuram Rajan, Professor of Finance at the University of Chicago and the current governor of the Reserve Bank of India (the Indian central bank), argue that the US sub-prime mortgage market was driven in part by the federal government and quasi-government federal agencies (see **Fannie Mae and Freddie Mac**) deciding to boost home ownership across the US as a strategic response to stagnant wages and rising income inequality. The Community Reinvestment Act (1977) had required banks to lend in their local markets, especially in lower-income, predominantly black areas. In 2000, the Clinton administration cut the minimum deposit required for a borrower to qualify for a government-guaranteed mortgage to 3 per cent, increased the maximum size of mortgage it would guarantee, and halved the premiums it charged borrowers for the guarantee. All these actions set the stage for a boom in low-income housing construction and lending (Rajan, 2010, p 37). Although not all the frenzied lending in the run-up to the credit crunch was related to low-income housing, there was a government-orchestrated expansion in mortgage lending to the less well-off (Rajan, 2010, p 40).[1]

Mark Blyth's analysis, on the other hand, largely exonerates states or governments, and focuses on four quintessentially private sector phenomena that made the credit crunch and ensuing financial crash possible: the US repo market as the 'generator' of the liquidity crunch; the part played by **credit derivatives** – CDOs and CDS – in spreading the repo crisis into the global banking system; the role played by **tail risk** in amplifying these problems; and the damage done by a set of economic ideas – the efficient markets hypothesis – that blinded bankers and regulators to the risks building up in the system.

As house prices fell and mortgage defaults increased in late 2006, the repo market could not absorb the volume of securities being dumped on it all at the same time by banks seeking to raise cash. But it needed derivatives – MBS and CDOs combined with CDS – to amplify the liquidity crunch into a system-wide financial crisis. By the mid-2000s, the market was awash with these new derivatives that bundled together the mortgage payments of many different bits of real estate, from many different parts of the US, and insured them with a CDS.

This became a problem because the banks were running out of good borrowers to whom they could lend, so later batches of these securities were increasingly made up of so-called 'ninja' (no income, no job, no assets) mortgages, and the banks issuing them, knowing full well their dubious quality, dumped them onto the conduits and SPVs to get them off their books. With each bank holding similar assets and liabilities, and each attempting to rid itself of these supposedly uncorrelated mortgage assets all at once, CDO prices collapsed. In September 2008, when the scope of CDS protection both written by and written on Lehman by firms such as AIG (American International Group, North America's largest insurance company) became apparent, not only did the markets take fright, but for the first time US policy-makers began to see the problem as systemic, and 'too big to fail' became a reality (Blyth, 2013, pp 23-31). First, AIG was bailed out, then the US Congress enacted TARP (the Troubled Asset Relief Program) that used US taxpayers' money to buy up the banks' bad debts.[2]

Beyond the fact that they chose not to regulate derivative markets, the financial crisis was not of governments' or states' making (Blyth, 2013, p 26). There is no disputing, however, that the depth of the crisis was directly related to residential mortgages having become such a central component of financial markets, although there were other contributory factors.[3] The rapid effect of the collapse in the US mortgage market on the wider US economy was seen between mid-2007 and the end of 2008, as over three million jobs were lost (over one million in manufacturing), the S&P share index fell by 40 per cent and – with the market value of their homes and retirement assets declining fast – households lost US$14 trillion (22 per cent) of their net worth (Panitch and Gindin, 2013, p 318).

From the global banking crisis to sovereign debt and austerity

The banking crisis quickly mutated into a fiscal crisis (the inability of national governments to raise enough tax revenue to pay for their planned spending programmes) as a result of the bank bailouts; and then, in some countries (particularly some Eurozone countries), into a **sovereign debt** crisis (a failure by the government of a sovereign state to persuade its creditors – often the self-same beneficiaries of the bank rescues – that it can pay back its outstanding debt).

For countries in the Eurozone periphery – Portugal, Ireland, Italy, Greece and Spain (the so-called PIIGS) – already deeply indebted after years of weakening competitiveness relative to the Eurozone core – rising fiscal deficits since 2010 have led to restricted access to international bond markets, to falling prices of government bonds and (the CDS market having emerged as an instrument for trading and speculating against the risk of a country defaulting) to widening sovereign CDS spreads relative to the core. Portugal's debt to GDP ratio, for example, increased from 62 per cent in 2006 to 108 per cent in 2012, while the yield on its 10-year bonds (the interest Portugal has to pay to get someone to hold its debt) went from 4.5 per cent in May 2009 to 14.7 per cent in January 2012 (Blyth, 2013, p 4).

In the same way that peripheral euro-governments' bonds became less attractive to the bond markets, so, too, private sector lending to the big European banks (mainly French and German) with lots of exposure to peripheral sovereign debt dried up in the summer and autumn of 2011. The European Central Bank's (ECB) response was to provide emergency liquidity assistance to the core euro-banks through long-term refinancing operations (LTRO). While these bank bailouts averted a credit crunch, they failed to stop speculative attacks on the sovereign bonds of peripheral euro-member states.

Mark Blyth argues that the Eurozone crisis is not really a 'sovereign debt' crisis at all but a banking crisis caused by the excessive exposure of 'core' euro-country banks to, initially, risky US sub-prime mortgage bonds and then, as these bonds' credit rating went from AAA to BBB and worse, to the sovereign bonds of peripheral euro-states, which they used as collateral for short-term funding in the US repo market. What happened in the US in 2007-08, a general liquidity crunch, gathered pace in Europe in 2010 and 2011, and was only averted by the ECB injecting a billion euros of cheap money, the LTROs, in late 2011 and early 2012, when European banks were no longer able to borrow money in the US. But within two months of the first LTRO, sovereign bond yields were rising again, and the banks the sovereigns were responsible for had even more debt on their hands.

The heart of the problem, as Blyth sees it, is that in each country, and across the Eurozone as a whole, European banks have become 'too big to bail'. No Eurozone sovereign can bail out a bank with exposures of the magnitude of the systemically important European banks that, according to the ratings agency Standard & Poor's, have cross-border exposures to creditors in peripheral countries that far exceed their capital adequacy requirement under the Basel Accords. French banks alone had some US$493 billion in exposures to the PIIGS, equivalent to 20 per cent of France's GDP (Blyth, 2013, pp 85-9, 254).

Beginning with Greece in 2010, governments of the countries most severely affected by the loss of market confidence have obtained a series of bailouts from the 'Troika' of the European Commission (responsible for implementing EU policies and spending EU funds), the ECB and the IMF, enabling them to refinance their public debt. These state bailouts have been accompanied by austerity programmes and 'structural adjustment' measures that have induced deep recessions.[4]

The Troika is insulated from democratic politics, and 'troikisation' has underlined the extent to which the Eurozone crisis is a crisis of democracy as much as it is a financial and economic crisis. Cobbled together in April 2010 as an emergency ad hoc economic directorate to take over control of the Greek economy and impose austerity measures as a condition of Greece obtaining its first loan from the temporary European Financial Stabilisation Facility (EFSF), the Troika is now inscribed into the European Stability Mechanism (ESM), the Eurozone's permanent bailout fund set up in 2012 for struggling Eurozone economies and banks.

To that extent, and for the duration of the loan(s), the Troika effectively governs those smaller countries – Greece, Portugal, Ireland and Cyprus – that have drawn on ESM funds to recapitalise their banks. The Troika issues 'memoranda of understanding' on the same model as the IMF, which dictate every detail of the member states' legislative programmes (Watkins, 2013). Spain has also received ESM funding but was able to negotiate a lesser degree of policy conditionality: the government retained some freedom of movement and did not have to sign a Memorandum (Malgesine, 2014).

In many countries, bank rescues have also been accompanied by **quantitative easing (QE)**, an unconventional form of monetary policy used by central banks to stimulate their economies when standard monetary policy has become ineffective, involving the purchase of financial assets from the banks (so helping to rebuild their balance sheets).[5]

The Bank of England sees the effect of QE as follows:

> … direct injections of money into the economy, primarily by buying gilts, can have a number of effects. The sellers of the assets (institutions such as banks, insurance companies and pension funds) have more money so may go out and spend it. That will help to boost growth. Or they may buy other assets instead, such as shares or company bonds. That will push up the prices of those assets, making the people who own them, either directly or through their pension funds, better off. So they may go out and spend more. And higher asset prices mean lower yields, which brings down the cost of borrowing for businesses and households. That should provide a further boost to spending. (Bank of England, nd)

But QE has also been cited as a major reason why UK company pension scheme deficits have ballooned. This is because the cost of paying pensions from final salary schemes is calculated on the assumption that all their assets are invested in bonds. By buying up government bonds, the Bank of England created a demand for them, so their price went up and their yield went down. As the yield on bonds has dropped, so the stock of assets needed to generate the same level of pension income has gone up. In May 2012, the aggregate UK pension scheme deficit reached a record high of £312 billion. If this persists, it will have to be paid off by employers, presenting them with a very large bill. Meanwhile, the fall in bond yields has driven down the annual income someone can obtain by buying an annuity with their accumulated pension pot. So anyone retiring and trying to buy a private pension in the past year or two has lost potential income that they will never get back (BBC News, 2013).

Ha-Joon Chang (2013) argues that QE has become the post-credit crunch weapon of choice in the UK, the US and some other developed countries such as Japan because it is the only way in which recovery – however slow and anaemic – can be generated without changing the model of economic growth that has served the rich and powerful so well since the 1980s. Chang accepts that in its initial phase, QE may have acted like an electric shock to someone who has just had a cardiac arrest. But subsequently, its boosting effects have been largely through the creation of unsustainable asset bubbles, in the stock market, in property markets and in commodity markets, bubbles that may burst and generate another round of financial crises.[6]

Banking reform

We might reasonably have expected a financial crisis of this magnitude to pose a fundamental challenge to neoliberal ideas and policies. Certainly, in the attempt to rebalance increasingly financialised economies (see **financialisation**) away from speculative trading towards the real economy in the wake of the financial crash, various proposals or measures have been introduced to reduce excess bank leverage and to increase lending to small and medium-sized businesses, the main source of innovation in the real economy. Yet to date, these reforms are generally considered to have been inadequate, slow and incomplete, with the proportion of profits from quick trades in the financial sector, rather than long-term investments, rising, not falling

(Mazzucato, 2014). Meanwhile, the neoliberal ideas that have failed the test of the great financial crash still walk among us (Quiggin, 2010).

The deregulated banks at the heart of the crisis have demonstrated their power to delay and/or substantially water down proposed reforms such as the EU's financial transactions tax on stocks, bonds, currencies and derivatives, modelled on the 'Tobin tax' – a worldwide levy on speculative currency transactions championed by the US economist James Tobin (1918-2002), designed to reduce excessive risk-taking by market traders. The global financial system still retains many of its essential features: a system marked by inordinate complexity, by opacity in modes of trading and by dangerously high levels of interconnectedness (Moran, 2013). Indeed, as a result of mergers and acquisitions, the system is now more concentrated than ever in the hands of a few LCFIs or G-SIBs. Banking scandals continue apace: since 2008, total fines levied in Europe and the US for banking crimes and misdemeanours top £100 billion, with banks making provision for a further £60 billion (Hutton, 2014). These crimes and misdemeanours include money laundering, the manipulation of foreign exchange rates, the fixing of the London Interbank Offered Rate (LIBOR) (see 'money markets') and the mis-selling of payment protection insurance (PPI) policies (Sikka, 2014).

In the US, where many commentators believe that the repeal of **Glass-Steagall** in 1999 contributed to the 2008 financial crash by ensuring that there was a demand for the kind of returns that could be obtained only through leverage and big risk-taking,[7] Title VII of the Dodd-Frank Act 2010 aimed to reduce systemic risk through mandating central clearing of previously unregulated derivative instruments, and by requiring more collateral to back derivative trades.

Among other provisions, Dodd-Frank mandated comprehensive reporting of 'over the counter' (OTC) trades (see 'derivatives'), and required public reporting of the prices at which the majority of derivatives are executed, but it did not bring the CDS market in line with the life insurance market by banning the sale of CDS in which the contracting party does not own the underlying asset(s), as many reformers had advocated. The Dodd-Frank provisions on derivatives largely left it to regulators to work out the details, and it was not long before the US Treasury announced that the most commonly used derivatives – foreign exchange swaps and forwards (used to hedge against fluctuations in currency values) – would be exempt from the rules because additional regulation might have serious negative consequences on global trade and capital flows (Panitch and Gindin, 2013, p 323).

However, in the US, banks that have an implicit government guarantee (that is, those that are seen as 'too big to fail') are no longer able to engage in certain types of proprietary trading. This is a practice that attracted considerable public notoriety in 2009 when it was reported that from 2004 to 2008, Goldman Sachs had encouraged its clients to invest in CDOs while at the same time betting its own money that CDOs would fall in value – by conspiring with hedge funds to 'short' them (see **short selling**) (Davies, 2010, pp 161-2).

The final version of what is known as the Volcker Rule (developed to implement Section 619 of Dodd-Frank and named after the former chairman of the Federal Reserve [Fed] who championed it) prohibits deposit-making banks and affiliated institutions ('banking entities') from engaging in short-term proprietary trading of certain securities, derivatives, commodity futures and options for their own account (see US SEC, 2013). The final set of rules also imposes limits on banking entities' investments in, and other relationships with, hedge funds or private equity funds, and limits the liabilities that the largest banks can hold (by tightening limits on acquisitions that would give banks 10 per cent or more of the liabilities in the US banking system). Banks are allowed to continue offering services such as underwriting, investment management advice, trading of government securities and insurance activities.[8]

In the UK, the incoming coalition government set up an Independent Commission on Banking (ICB), which recommended that UK banks should ring-fence their retail operations from their investment banking activities, and that the banks' capital reserve requirements should be tightened. The Commission did, however, reject the idea of a full split, rather than a ring fence, on the grounds that the diversity of businesses within a large group and the diversification of their assets might improve stability in a crisis. The UK government subsequently brought in legislation (the Banking Reform Act 2013) in line with the Commission's proposals (Wolf, 2014, p 230). As recommended by the ICB, banks are required to have implemented the new arrangements by 2019. The delay in implementation has been justified on the grounds that there is a real tension between, on the one hand, trying to boost the total amount of demand to get the economy out of recession and, on the other, making the banking system more safe and secure (Bootle, 2012, pp 227-8).[9]

Notes

[1]   The Financial Crisis Inquiry Commission found that Fannie Mae and Freddie Mac had, for decades, used their political power to ward off effective regulation and oversight, and that they had ramped up their exposure to sub-prime mortgages as the housing market was peaking in 2005 and 2006. Fannie and Freddie's purchases of MBS were financed by huge borrowing and they were 'the kings of leverage': by the end of 2007, their combined leverage ratio, including loans they owned and guaranteed, stood at 75:1 (Financial Crisis Inquiry Commission, 2011, p xx). But during most of the housing bubble they had been rapidly losing market share because banks were taking on borrowers, in particular sub-prime borrowers, that the government-sponsored agencies would not touch (Krugman, 2012, p 65). In other words, Fannie and Freddie followed rather than led Wall Street and other lenders in the rush for fool's gold (Financial Crisis Inquiry Commission, 2011, p xxvi).

When, in September 2008, they were put under the direct control ('conservatorship') of the federal government and bailed out with US$189.5 billion of public money, Fannie and Freddie had US$5.4 trillion of MBS and debt outstanding, a sum equal to the entire official debt of the US. Between 35 and 40 per cent of the debt issued as bonds was held by other countries' central banks (Thompson, 2009, p 18).

Conservatorship itself, it has been argued, was less a *rescue* than a *seizure* or confiscation of shareholders' stakes in Fannie and Freddie by a dogmatic, free-market Republican administration intent on closing down the two government-sponsored enterprises. Among the confiscated shareholders were several foreign governments and sovereign wealth funds (see 'bonds') that had provided badly need capital to US financial institutions throughout the credit crunch (Kaletsky, 2010, p 143).

[2] TARP was a US federal government programme approved by Congress in October 2008 to purchase or insure up to US$700 billion in assets and equity from financial and other institutions. Although not described as such, this amounted to the 'nationalisation' of the troubled banks whose assets were purchased. TARP was hugely controversial, and when the House of Representatives voted down the original measure in what Timothy Garton Ash describes as a collision between the urgent demands of the contemporary American version of democracy and those of the contemporary American version of capitalism, it was House Republicans who defied President Bush's appeal for support for the bailout. For some, the choice was ideological; they would rather die than vote for an expansion of government's role in the US economy (Garton Ash, 2008).

The Dodd-Frank Act later reduced the US$700 billion authorisation to US$475 billion. A total of US$245 billion went to stabilise banks, US$27 billion went to programmes to increase credit availability, US$80 billion went to the US car industry (specifically to GM and Chrysler), US$68 billion went to stabilise AIG, and US$46 billion went to foreclosure prevention programmes. TARP rules banned companies benefiting from the federal government bailout from awarding bonuses to their top 25 highest-paid executives. When wrapping up TARP in December 2013, the US Department of the Treasury stated that the programme had earned more than US$11 billion for taxpayers (Investopedia, Troubled Asset Relief Program).

[3] Economist and former editor at large of *The Times* (of London) newspaper Anatole Kaletsky argues that the financial crisis was just a typical financial bust exacerbated by gross policy errors. For example, **mark to market accounting** was suspended by US regulatory authorities in March 2009. Had this been done six months earlier, the sequence of events leading up to the crash could probably have been confined to a normal financial downturn, accompanied, in the real economy, by nothing worse than a moderate slowdown in economic growth (Kaletsky, 2010, p 141).

[4] Keynesian stimulus policies were briefly in vogue in the immediate aftermath of the global financial crash of 2008 but came to an abrupt end when pro-austerity politicians in the UK, US and Germany seized on the 2010 Greek debt crisis as a metaphor for the perils of profligate, Keynesian-style deficit spending (Blyth, 2013, p 72).

[5] Effectively the LTROs are an ECB version of QE, with the ECB flooding the banks with cheap loans and the banks then lending this money to governments at considerably higher interest rates (Laskarides, 2014, p 79).

[6] Inspired by the ancient Judeo-Christian idea of 'jubilee' – a time, once every 50 years, when debts were cancelled, slaves were freed and land was redistributed – the Australian economist Steve Keen has proposed the

introduction of a 'modern debt jubilee', taking the form of 'quantitative easing for the public' (QEP). A modern jubilee would involve the Bank of England or US Fed creating new money in the same way as with QE, but transferring it not into the reserve accounts of banks and other financial institutions, but, at the request of the government (technically, such transfers count as fiscal policy, which falls outside the purview of central bankers):

> ... into the bank accounts of the public with the requirement that the first use of this money would be to reduce debt. Debtors whose debt exceeded their (cash) injection would have their debt reduced but not eliminated, while recipients with no debt would receive a cash injection into their deposit accounts to spend as they wish. Bank assets would remain constant in value, but their distribution would alter with debt-instruments declining in value and cash assets rising. Bank income would fall since debt is an income-earning asset for a bank while cash reserves are not. (Keen, 2012, p 18)

Nor is the argument for a debt jubilee a new one (the *doyen* of free market economists, Milton Friedman, first conjured up the image of bank notes dropping from the skies in 1969), but until recently, the idea of the government transferring new money created by the central bank direct to households as cash deposits in their bank accounts – as opposed to the central bank printing money to buy financial assets from banks for them in turn to lend the money to businesses or to private investors (QE) – has remained taboo in conventional policy circles (Turner, 2013; Blyth and Lonergan, 2014).

Ironically, and perhaps fittingly, the compensation payments imposed on the banks by UK regulators for mis-selling payment protection insurance policies (which provide cover against the risk of default on mortgage, credit card or loan repayments) are themselves a form of 'helicopter money': millions of people have lodged a formal PPI complaint and the £16 billion paid out to date in refunds is an economic boost equivalent to 1 per cent of GDP (Peston, 2014).

[7] In truth, the repeal was more symbolic than a direct cause of the behaviour that led to the crash, as much of the substance of Glass-Steagall had already been eroded.

[8] The Volcker Rule has led to an exodus of top proprietary traders from the big banks to form their own hedge funds or to join existing ones, which, as non-deposit-taking institutions, do not enjoy any implicit government guarantee (Wikipedia, Volcker Rule).

[9] The US economist and former external member of the Bank of England's Monetary Policy Committee, Adam Posen, is one of a growing number of influential critics who have argued that there is an urgent need to address

more fundamental deficiencies in the UK financial system. In his view, the City of London has far better served global finance than British domestic business, and the UK needs to create a diversity of lending sources to increase investment in small and medium-sized businesses that are unable to access credit from the five main 'high street' commercial banks (Posen, 2013). So, too, Richard Werner, Professor of International Banking at the University of Southampton, has forcefully argued the case for small, community-based credit unions and local authority owned-banks in the UK, based on the German model: banks which account for 70 per cent of the banking sector in that country and have no interest in speculative credit creation (Werner, 2012).

THREE

Putting the great financial crash in its place

Let them eat credit. (Rajan, 2010, p 21)

A different sort of crisis

Nearly a decade on from what was initially framed as a 'credit crunch' or a problem confined to the financial markets, it is abundantly clear that the great financial crash was no ordinary 'boom and bust', but a more profound crisis *of* capitalism, with the potential to bring about new policies, political alignments and ideologies (Gamble, 2009). If we are to understand what is new and distinctive about the 2008 crash and its aftershocks, compared to other more run-of-the-mill financial crises, we need to set the complex and often dramatic events outlined in Chapters One and Two in their wider historical and ideological context. This is the purpose of this present chapter, which outlines a number of distinct stages of capitalist growth and development since 1945.

This entails a switch of focus away from 'finance' to political economy, with this chapter becoming, in effect, a guide to the wider political and economic context in which the global financial crisis should be understood. It also means engaging with some 'big picture' theorising about how and why capitalist economies evolve across time and space. The 'big picture' analysis set out in this chapter draws on the ideas and concepts of the 'regulation school', a group of academic writers on political economy whose work, in my view, provides real insight into both the crisis-prone nature of modern capitalist democracies and the breakdown of a particular mode of ordering or stabilising the current era of finance-led capitalism in the US and the UK – 'privatised Keynesianism' (reliance on the private, credit-financed debt of low- to middle-income households to stimulate economic growth rather than public debt) – without which an understanding of the 2008 crash is incomplete.

There is a flipside to big picture theorising, which is that it requires generalisation and abstraction. So let's start with a word of warning. In seeking to present a simplified, if highly abstract picture of reality, regulationists, along with many other social scientists, make use of 'ideal types' as a way of conceptualising or describing something – for example, the transition from Fordism to neo- or post-Fordism – that is derived from observable reality but does not conform to it in detail because of deliberate simplification and exaggeration. This way of making sense of something is often confusing to the layperson, and it is important to bear in mind that an ideal type is not ideal in the sense that it is excellent. It is, rather, a constructed ideal used to approximate reality by selecting and accentuating certain elements (see www. britannica.com, 'ideal type'). Another problem with the regulation school has already been noted in the Introduction: its members have an unfortunate penchant for writing in an academic vernacular that makes their work more or less inaccessible to outsiders.

The rest of this book, then, is only tangentially concerned with the ways in which the banks could be made safer and healthier. Others with more expertise than myself have already written succinctly on this theme in clear, accessible language (see, for example, Admati and Hellwig, 2013; Davies; 2015). Rather, the intention here is to provide a clear route map of the path(s) already travelled by Western economies since 1945 (this chapter); to take a closer look at real-world variation in the Anglo-American heartland of neoliberalism, where the financial crisis originated (Chapter Four), and at the Eurozone sovereign debt crisis (Chapter Five); and to ask whether the crisis really is over, or whether, on the contrary, we may be in the early stages of a transition to a new type of capitalism (Chapter Six).

The great complacence

The credit crunch-turned-great financial crash of 2007-08 brought to an end a long period of growth and stability in the US, the UK and many other Western countries, albeit growth punctuated by periodic recessions and the bursting of financial bubbles, such as the Asian crash of 1997 and the dot.com crash of 2000. The general movement of financial markets was upwards and the general sentiment was optimistic. In the UK, the broad consensus is that the growth model adopted in the 1980s, whose main drivers were financial services, retail, property and construction in the private sector, and education, health and universities in the public sector, achieved considerable success in the 1990s and up to 2007 (Gamble, 2011).

Underlying this buoyancy was the impact of the entry of China and other rising powers, as well as the former communist states of the old Soviet Union, into the global economy. The flood of cheap imports which the former, in particular, made possible helped to keep inflation at low levels and sustained the consumer boom in the West, as did the development of ever more sophisticated financial instruments designed to expand and broaden access to credit, especially mortgage credit.

Many commentators have blamed the banks for the crisis, and in particular the investment banks (see, for example, Tett, 2009). Others have argued that the primary culprits were the politicians, who stood by and let debt levels rise remorselessly (Turner, 2008), or the regulators for not restraining the increasingly dubious lending practices of some parts of the housing and banking sectors (Davies, 2010). Some remarks made shortly before the credit crunch by Ben Bernanke, chair of the US Federal Reserve (Fed) from 2006 to 2014, point to another, very significant contributory factor:

In addressing the challenges and risks that financial innovation may create, we should also always keep in view the enormous economic benefits that flow from a healthy and innovative financial sector. The increasing sophistication and depth of financial markets promote economic growth by allocating capital where it is most productive. And the dispersion of risk more broadly across the financial system has, thus far, increased the resilience of the system and the economy to shocks. (Bernanke, 2007)

Bernanke's remarks epitomise the 'great complacence' about the Great Moderation – the apparent reduction in the volatility of business cycle fluctuations – that prevailed among regulators, academics, bankers, the media and politicians in the 25 years preceding the 2007 credit crunch (Engelen et al, 2011). Blindness to the growing fragility of the financial system operated in a frame of ideologies and interests that had, for four decades, increasingly undermined political questioning of, or resistance to, the rise of a financialised or finance-led economy, a trend enabled by the financial deregulation that began with the breakdown of the Bretton Woods system of fixed exchange rates in the early 1970s and intensified in the 1980s with the removal of most restrictions on international capital flows and exchange rate movements.

Bretton Woods was a landmark system for monetary and exchange rate management established in 1944, at a conference held in Bretton Woods in New Hampshire. Its terms were set by the US, the dominant global power - then as (if less securely) now – and its major outcomes were the introduction of an adjustable foreign exchange rate regime that pegged currencies to gold, and the creation of a new IMF to intervene when an imbalance of payments arose. Although gold initially served as the base reserve currency, the US dollar gained momentum as an international reserve currency that was convertible into gold, and against which other currencies came to be pegged at fixed rates (Investopedia, Bretton Woods Agreement). Under this system, governments were limited in the extent they could run persistent budget or trade deficits by the need to appease creditors (Coggan, 2012, p 256).

As noted in Chapter One, at the intellectual root of the great complacence was the mainstream economics profession's theory of efficient and rational markets, also known as the 'efficient markets hypothesis': that optimal outcomes will be achieved if the demand and supply for goods and services are allowed to adjust to each other through the price mechanism, with the best role for government being to do very little (Davies, 2010, p 180). The *intellectual* significance of the great financial crash is that it revealed these efficient market assumptions to be built on sand or, to switch metaphors, a case of the emperor's new clothes (Kynaston, 2012, p ix).

The regulation approach

Let's turn our attention to a very different perspective on the Great Moderation, the credit crunch and the 2008 crash: one that holds that these events can only be properly understood as the latest stages in a neoliberal developmental sequence that has transformed the nature of democratic capitalism, a political-economic formation which itself came to be more or less securely established only after the Second World War – and one which is marked by a continuing friction between the workings of the market economy and democratic politics (Streeck, 2014).

To put this developmental sequence itself into context, we'll rely on the periodisation proposed by a number of historians and social scientists, and divide up the economic history of the capitalist democracies of the rich West since 1945 into three distinct phases: post-war reconstruction (1945-50[1]); the era of 'organised' or 'managerial' capitalism (also known as the Keynesian 'golden age') and its subsequent disintegration (1950-75); and, following a period of transition, the era of neoliberal globalisation associated with the rise of finance-led capitalism (from 1979 onwards[2]) (Lash and Urry, 1987; Armstrong et al, 1991; Crouch, 2011). This section explores the second and third of these chronological phases through the lens of the 'regulation approach'.

The regulation approach, as developed by the French regulationist school in the 1970s, rejects the notion that capitalist economies are self-regulating and have an inherent tendency to return to equilibrium or a stable resting place. The school's central pre-occupation is with how the production and growth ('accumulation', in the academic vernacular) of the advanced capitalist democracies is *regularised* (or *normalised* or *ordered*) by a 'mode of regulation' which embeds this socially and politically.[3] Instead of assuming that development within national economies progresses along a smooth path, the regulation approach maintains that mechanisms and policies have to be put in place to overcome recurring fault lines over the distribution of wages and profits between capital and organised labour on the one hand, and between different types of capital (especially between manufacturing and finance capital) on the other.

It is precisely this set of assumptions about the crisis-prone nature of modern capitalist economies – and related assumptions about the importance of historically developed class relations and political and institutional forms in shaping the origins and consequences of such crises in specific national contexts – that are borne out by the historical record of longish phases of relative stability interrupted by periodic, systemic crises of capitalism.[4]

The regulation approach initially focused on the ability of countries associated with 'Atlantic Fordism'[5] (the US, north-western Europe, Canada, Australia and New Zealand) to secure a long period of stability during the post-war golden age despite Fordism's inherent tendency to instability, crisis and change. Later, in the 1980s, the focus on national regimes of accumulation was extended to developments in the international economy and to the emergence of a new type of financialised or finance-led capitalism.

Caricaturing and simplifying somewhat, Fordism or organised capitalism corresponds to the post-1950 era of mass production and mass consumption of manufactured goods involving large-scale investment in fixed plant and machinery. In what may be described as the political economy of Fordism, the link between mass production and mass consumption was regulated and sustained by institutionalised collective bargaining between capital and labour, and a system of protected national markets. The corresponding state form was the 'Keynesian welfare state', in which governments used the tax and expenditure powers of the state to secure full employment and to provide collectively financed welfare services to protect its citizens from the insecurities of the free market.

This era is sometimes referred to as 'managerial capitalism' in recognition of the power and influence exercised over decision-making at company level by managerial executives rather than by owners or shareholders. As such, the term signifies a form of organisational control in which labour, technology and administrative structures are coordinated by a cadre of salaried managers and related professionals with little or no equity ownership stake in the enterprises that they manage and direct (Galbraith, 1967; Chandler, 1984; Fleming, 2008).

Although there are several variants of the regulation approach,[6] all subscribe to the proposition that the stable relationship between production and consumption that allowed the capitalist democracies to sustain profits and investment in the era of organised capitalism broke down during the 'crossroad years' of the 1970s and early to mid-1980s, along with the set of public policies that served to regularise or normalise that relationship (Harris, 1988). The most fundamental shift was in the structure of production, consisting of the methods of production, the strategies of management and the relations between trade unions, employers and the state. The core thesis is that a decisive shift from Fordism to neo-Fordism (in some versions post-Fordism) was taking place during this period.[7]

Central to neo-Fordist production and growth is the development of flexible specialisation to replace the rigid assembly line system of production. Neo-Fordism is marked by more intense, global competition from flexible producers (initially Japanese firms) using new techniques of production and work organisation associated with the rise of information and communications technology (ICT) to manufacture a range of innovative products.

In this new growth regime, production is organised on a global basis, with the 'offshoring' of much manufacturing work to countries offering cheap and non-unionised labour, as well as less regulation and lower tax rates, often located within free or special zones (Urry, 2014, pp 29-30). Organised labour becomes weaker and a 'dual' economy develops, with an increasingly insecure peripheral or flexible workforce and a salaried core of managerial or professional employees who perform the vital activities of the global company.

The outstanding political development in the decade or so after 1975 was the break-up of the Keynesian 'social democratic' consensus, with right-wing parties adopting aggressive policies to redistribute income in favour of business, and workers' parties seeking to preserve the gains of the boom and ensure that the costs of slower growth and economic restructuring were broadly spread (Armstrong et al, 1991, p xv). Although the push toward the new neoliberal order may have come from giant firms operating on a global scale, and also from international organisations such as the IMF, its political ascendancy was secured by the ability of a new generation of crusading domestic politicians led by Margaret Thatcher and Ronald Reagan to sell the free market, neoliberal project to the UK and US electorates.

Regulationists endorse the view that the economic relations between countries since the end of the Second World War have rested on a US-led international market order based initially on Bretton Woods[8] and then, following President Nixon's decision (made at a time of rising inflation and slowing growth) to abandon the dollar's convertibility to gold in 1971, on floating exchange rates and the progressive liberalisation of trade and financial markets (Harris, 1988; Gamble, 2014). Unlike the fixed exchange rates and capital controls of the Bretton Woods order, floating exchange rates allowed larger trade deficits and greater international capital movements, as well as much greater swings in exchange rates, at least in the US dollar and the pound sterling.[9]

Free movement of capital and floating exchange rates changed the financial sector in two main ways. First, they created the need for companies and investors to protect themselves against currency risk, so facilitating derivatives trading and the development of financial futures markets. Second, the flow of capital across the globe created the need for bigger banks capable of making credit more widely available to a more diverse group of investors (Coggan, 2012, p 156).[10] These developments, facilitated by successive rounds of ICT-enabled innovation, have transformed not only the speed of financial transactions and the operation of financial markets, but also the nature of financial regulation. Previously tightly controlled, nationally organised and centred on commercial banking, the regulatory regime for money and banking became more self-regulated, global in reach, and centred on investment banking – a regime characterised by new ways to fund debt that seemingly enabled fluctuations in the business cycle to be smoothed out and much larger trade imbalances between countries to be accommodated during the years of the Great Moderation (Guttmann, 2008).

This is a qualitatively different type of capitalism that reflects the declining autonomy of nation states; the increasing economic weight and political influence of giant transnational corporations (particularly large, complex financial institutions), and the rising significance of city regions and 'world cities' such as New York, London and Tokyo.

Jamie Peck, a leading regulationist, distinguishes between two 'faces' of the third, finance-led, neoliberal phase of capitalism: 'roll back' and 'roll out'. The former is associated with the Thatcher-Reagan decade of the 1980s, its attacks on Keynesianism and organised labour, and its rolling back of state intervention in the economy through policies of deregulating markets and privatising state-owned enterprises. The 'roll out' face is marked by a number of features:

- Proactive state management of the tensions and consequences of the roll back face (rising household debt, increased unemployment and welfare dependency, widening inequalities of income and wealth). In particular, as described by Bob Jessop, 'workfare' (publicly funded programmes designed to get people back into work, where eligible recipients must be able to demonstrate that they are actively seeking to enter the labour market) is increasingly substituted for the more traditional 'welfare state' benefits providing protection against unemployment and invalidity (Jessop, 2002).

• The extension of market-complementing forms of regulation. The neoliberal state seeks to create a more competitive economy through recalibrating regulatory controls on business and stimulating innovation and enterprise. It becomes, in Jessop's (2002) phrase, a 'Schumpeterian' state. Particular attention is paid to 'supply side' approaches to employment growth based on a strategy of boosting productivity and stimulating demand for workers by creating more flexible labour markets, as opposed to traditional, Keynesian-style public spending programmes. This kind of strategy makes it easier for employers to hire and fire workers.[11] Local and regional tiers of government increasingly take on the characteristics of 'entrepreneurial' governments competing with each other to boost the formation and growth of new firms and, in the case of regions and larger cities, to attract internationally mobile capital.

• The shift towards more market-oriented public services and the growing involvement of private companies in their delivery, where relationships and behaviour are driven by competition and profit. In David Harvey's formulation, governmental and corporate activities become more 'porous' (Harvey, 2007, p 78). Financial institutions working in tandem with large civil engineering and construction firms became the driving force behind what in the UK has been termed the 'public services industry' (PSI) – an amalgam of private and voluntary (or 'third sector') enterprises that provide services to the public on behalf of government, or to the government itself (Julius, 2008, p 5) – centred, in the years leading up to the crash, on the private financing of public infrastructure projects such as new hospitals, schools and prisons.[12]

Importantly, there is no simple convergence over time and place on a single model of neoliberalism, but a variety of contextually specific *pathways of neoliberalisation*, reflecting different modes of national accommodation to the growing internationalisation of production, trade and finance (Peck, 2012, pp 19-27).

Financialisation again

If you've looked at the Appendix, you'll know that 'financialisation' is a term used to denote both the financialised economy (the tendency for profit-making to occur increasingly through financial channels rather than through productive activities) and the penetration of finance and 'finance thinking' into increasing areas of everyday life. Here we pick up on one particular dimension of the first meaning of financialisation: the emergence in the Anglo-American heartland of a new form of corporate governance (the system of rules, practices and processes by which business corporations are directed and controlled) focused on maximising shareholder value,[13] which places a premium on short-term profits over long-term growth, sustainability and employment (Lazonick, 2009). We pick up on a second dimension – the systematic encouragement of households to take on more debt – in the next section.

Under organised/managerial capitalism or the 'old economy' business model characterised by career employment with one employer, returns on investment were based on the value created by productive enterprises, and employees were rewarded with a stable job, salary increases and retirement security. Similarly, under the 'old economy' business model that was dominant in high-tech companies coming into the 1980s, profits were reinvested in the workforce, and employees were able to contribute to innovation by learning about the company's proprietary technologies, many of which had been developed in its corporate research laboratories.

But the advent of non-proprietary technologies, associated initially with Silicon Valley, meant that 'old economy' companies now had to compete for talent with 'new economy' start-ups that used stock options to persuade high-tech workers to give up secure employment with the established companies. Under this new regime, the stock market was elevated to a position of far greater influence over the allocation of corporate resources than ever before, and executive pay became increasingly stock-based. By the decade beginning in 2000, the shareholder focus had diffused broadly across the whole economy, and companies had come to be seen as vehicles for maximising financial returns regardless of geographic location or the implications for domestic employment (Appelbaum and Batt, 2010; Lazonick, 2010; Parramore, 2014).

Rather than retaining corporate earnings and reinvesting them in the business and in wage returns to workers, the logic of financialisation or financialised corporate resource allocation is to downsize the workforce and distribute corporate earnings disproportionately to shareholders and senior corporate executives (Martin et al, 2014, p 8). Corporate profits that could have been spent on innovation and job creation to replace lost middle-class jobs have instead been used to pay out higher dividends and to inflate share prices through companies buying back their own shares.[14] Research by the US economic historian Bill Lazonick has demonstrated that these payouts and buy-backs have had an adverse impact on the cost and quality of products in a range of industries such as oil refining, ICT, pharmaceuticals and banking, undermining the prosperity of the US economy (Lazonick, 2013, pp 859-60).

Among the biggest stock re-purchasers in the years prior to the great financial crash were the major investment banks that were bailed out under TARP, and leading ICT companies such as Microsoft, IBM, Cisco Systems, Intel and Hewlett-Packard. Over this period, all these companies exported high-tech jobs to lower-wage parts of the world such as China and India while using the profits of outsourcing to undertake stock buy-backs at home (Lazonick, 2010, pp 695-8).

Yet it would be a mistake, notwithstanding the lost jobs and the manipulation of share prices through massive stock repurchases, to draw the conclusion that the financialised US economy is no longer competitively engaged in manufacturing. The assertion of shareholder value should not blind us to the important role played by financial markets in expanding the availability of relatively cheap credit for US firms, in pushing inefficient firms out of business and in supporting high-tech start-ups through the US' venture capital markets,[15] whose disbursements grew 10-fold in the 1980s alone (Panitch and Gindin, 2013, p 188):

> Shored up by its high-tech sectors, during 1983-99 US manufacturing output grew faster (4.2 per cent annually) than overall GDP (3.7 per cent).... This enormous productivity growth was reflected in a rise in overall manufacturing volume of 90 per cent over the same period, whilst manufacturing employment showed virtually no increase at all (of the 34.4 million private sector jobs created in the US over this period, 99 per cent were outside manufacturing).The trajectory of the computer and peripheral equipment sector captures this well: it achieved an astonishing annual increase in real output of 29 per cent throughout the 1990s; but with productivity growing at the even more extraordinary rate of 31 per cent, there was no net job growth. (Panitch and Gindin, 2013, p 191)

Privatised Keynesianism

Following Colin Crouch (2011), what we have witnessed over the past 20 years or so in the new era of finance-led capitalism is a form of 'privatised Keynesianism': instead of governments taking on debt to stimulate the economy (post-war Keynesianism), low- to middle-income individuals have done so *en masse* via cheap credit cards and mortgages.

Privatised Keynesianism was made possible by the innovations that took place in financial markets in the 1990s, notably, the rapid growth of securitisation. The debt model is central to both original (welfare) and privatised Keynesianism, and both can be seen as attempts to reconcile the need for manufacturing and finance capital to have a mass consumer base. One does it through government fiscal (tax and spend) policy, the other through individual credit consumption, but whereas the regulated capitalism of the Keynesian period saw wage growth and a gradual reduction in inequalities of income and wealth in all advanced countries, the period following the 1970s inflationary crisis of the Keynesian model has brought the highest rewards to the class of financial intermediaries who have dealt in the regime of largely deregulated financial markets instituted since the 1980s. 'We now know', writes Crouch, 'that two very different forces came together to rescue the neoliberal model from the instability that would otherwise have been its fate: the growth of credit markets for poor and middle-income people, and the emergence of derivatives and futures markets among the very wealthy' (Crouch, 2011, p 114).

In the US and the UK, this combination produced a debt-based system that occurred initially by chance, but which gradually became a crucial matter for public policy insofar as it enabled mass consumption to be sustained in the absence of secure employment and secure labour markets. But the consumer debt model is also crucial to those national economies such as Germany and Japan that depend on exports rather than domestic consumption to fuel growth as they, and newly producing countries such as China, require the US and UK consumer to buy their goods. In both types of economy, therefore, public policy has been bearing down on wages to keep prices low: in the Anglophone countries, by reducing collective labour rights that might interfere with markets; in Germany and some other European countries, through the anti-inflationary stance of the ECB (Crouch, 2011, p 115).

The *practical* significance of the great financial crash is that it marks the breakdown of privatised Keynesianism as a hitherto successful method of reconciling finance-led capitalism with growing inequality in the distribution of income and life chances, a theme that we take up in the next chapter.

Notes

[1]   Post-war recovery in Europe owed a great deal to the Marshall Plan (1948-51), announced by the US Secretary of State George Marshall in 1947, which channelled some US$13 billion (equivalent to US$130 billion today) into the war-torn economies of Europe. Marshall Aid financed essential imports and the rebuilding of infrastructure but, more importantly, it was a political

signal that the US saw it in its own interest that other nations, including its former enemies, prosper (although the Marshall Plan was confined to Europe, a similar shift of policy towards Japan soon followed). The US also took the lead in establishing the General Agreement on Tariffs and Trade (GATT), which allowed developing countries to protect their domestic producers more actively than richer countries (Armstrong et al, 1999, pp 68-80; Chang, 2007, pp 62-4).

[2] 1979 is a more or less arbitrary starting point for the third phase, chosen because it is the year in which Margaret Thatcher became the UK's first female prime minister and abolished exchange controls on the movement of the domestic and foreign currencies in or out of the country.

[3] Unfortunately, this sense of regularisation is lost by the literal translation of *régulation* into English as 'regulation', with its connotation of a regime of controls over the operation of financial and other markets of the sort encountered in Chapter One. (The French word for regulation in this narrower sense is *réglementation*.)

[4] These assumptions are widely shared by economists and social scientists, Keynesians in particular, who reject free market fundamentalism. They include informed observers such as Anatole Kaletsky (2010) who see capitalism as evolving from one phase to the next but have a more benign view of the capitalist system and attach less significance than do the early regulationists to the key role of class conflict in shaping the dynamics of capitalist growth. Bob Jessop, a leading contemporary regulationist, accepts that over time the regulation approach has experienced a certain loss of identity through mutual interaction with other 'radical' approaches to capitalism and/or capitalist societies (Jessop and Sum, 2006, p 3).

[5] The term 'Fordism' is named after Henry Ford (1863-1947), who pioneered modern assembly-line production with his Model T car.

[6] The regulation approach has some affinities with an alternative 'neo-Schumpeterian' approach that also attaches importance to the instability of capitalism and to the role played by crises in initiating new cycles of economic development, but is distinctive in the importance it attributes to processes of 'creative destruction' in renewing and reinvigorating capitalism. This approach is named after the Austrian economist Joseph Schumpeter (1883-1950), whose influential model of capitalism stressed the importance of 'entrepreneurship' and continuous technological and organisational innovation in promoting the conditions for business success and the overall health of the capitalist economy. Schumpeter himself believed that as capitalism evolved, the intellectual and social climate needed to allow entrepreneurship to thrive would break down, paving the way for (a democratic form of) socialism.

[7] The term *neo*-Fordism emphasises the intensification of existing mass production in the face of global competition, rather than its demise (*post*-Fordism). While this terminology continues to be used in the social science literature, neo- or post-Fordism has been largely replaced as a concept for analysing the world of work and employment relations in the current neoliberal era by more fashionable concepts such as 'lean production' (new systems of work organisation introduced by employers to improve productivity, quality and profitability) and the shift from an 'old economy' to a 'new economy' business model (see, for example, Lazonick, 2009).

[8] Bretton Woods can be seen as the most systematic effort to manage or 'organise' contemporary capitalism in a period in which international economic developments were becoming increasingly significant (Lash and Urry, 1987, p 203).

[9] The countries in the European Exchange Rate Mechanism (ERM) continued to operate a 'semi-pegged' system of fixed exchange rates based on the European currency unit (ECU), with rates that were variable within certain margins. The ERM was introduced in 1979 to reduce exchange rate volatility and achieve monetary stability in Europe, in preparation for the switch to a single currency, the euro, which took place in 1999. The UK entered the ERM in 1990 but was forced to withdraw in 1992 after the pound sterling came under major pressure from currency speculators.

[10] Writing in 1982, the Paris-based regulationist Michel Aglietta described the emergence of 'a fully-fledged international credit system (that was) deterritorialised and beyond recognition by any sovereign state' (Aglietta, 1982, as quoted in Urry, 2014, p 61). Aglietta was referring to the extensive growth of the 'offshore' money markets of the eurodollar system of lending by European financial institutions to US companies in amounts denominated in US dollars. The term 'eurodollar' originally referred to US dollars in European banks, but its meaning has expanded over the years to its present definition of US dollar-denominated deposits in banks outside the US: similar deposits in Tokyo or Beijing would also be deemed eurodollar deposits. There is no connection with the euro currency (Wikipedia, Eurodollar).

[11] A second approach to employment policy rests more on improving people's prospects of employment by enhancing and upgrading their skills and general employability.

[12] Stephen Wilks has described the PSI as a 'new corporate state' where a distinct corporate sector (one that specialises in winning government contracts) has become as influential as the departments and agencies of government itself, delivering public services outside all the safeguards, expectations and due processes of British government (Wilks, 2013). The prototype was the private finance initiative (PFI), introduced in 1992 by

the Conservative government of John Major. Designated as a 'public–private partnership', its key feature was that the government used private finance to fund public infrastructure projects rather than raise the money through the bond market. Under PFI, the private sector partner raises the finance and the public authority makes a stream of annual payments to the consortium that finances, designs and operates the project and related services.

[13] We focus here on the US. Readers wishing to know more about comparable developments in the UK, particularly the peculiar cultural indifference to predatory foreign takeovers of British companies, are recommended to consult Will Hutton's hard-hitting *How good we can be* (2015), especially Chapter 3. See also John Kay's *Review of UK equity markets and long-term decision making* (2012).

[14] Dividends paid to stockholders (shareholders) rose as a share of the profits of US non-financial corporations from an average of 32 per cent between 1960 and 1980 to almost 60 per cent between 1981 and 2007 (Panitch and Gindin, 2013, p 187). For example, in 2004 General Motors, one of America's best-known companies, made 80 per cent of its profits from its financial division. It also spent US$20.4 billion on share buy-backs between 1986 and 2002 (Sayer, 2015, p 195). In contrast, compensation/ remuneration in the form of stocks and stock options was practically non-existent in Europe until the 1990s, except in the UK. Even in 2008, only 19 per cent of the compensation of European corporate executives was in the form of stock options and stock-related incentives (Conyon and Sadler, 2010).

[15] *Venture capital* is related to private equity, but instead of buying existing companies, venture capitalists invest in start-up companies with perceived long-term growth potential in exchange for an equity stake in the start-up (Scott, 2013, p 83). Venture capital funds raise money from institutional and other investors – insurance companies, pension funds, educational endowments and wealthy individuals sometimes known as angel investors – whose investment portfolios typically include a small percentage allocation to alternative investment classes. The creation of Nasdaq (National Association of Securities Dealers Automated Quotations, now the second largest stock exchange in the US) in 1971 as an electronic stock market whose listing requirements were far less stringent than those on the 'old economy' New York Stock Exchange provided venture capitalist firms with the possibility of a relatively quick exit from their investment in start-ups, inducing a flow of organised venture capital into what would become the 'new economy' (Lazonick, 2010, pp 694-5).

FOUR

Exploring the neoliberal heartland

There are definitely two Americas. I live in one, on one block in Baltimore that is part of the viable America, the America that is connected to its own economy, where there is a plausible future for the people born into it. About 20 blocks away is another America entirely. It's astonishing how little we have to do with each other.... That may be the ultimate tragedy of capitalism in our time, that it has achieved its dominance without regard to a social compact, without being connected to any other metric for human progress. ('There are now two Americas. My country is a horror show', *The Guardian*, 8 December 2013, edited extract from a speech by David Simon, creator of the HBO series *The Wire*, to the Festival of Dangerous Ideas in Sydney, Australia; reproduced courtesy of Guardian News & Media Ltd)

Real regulation: institutions, interests and ruling ideas

So far, so abstract, you may well be forgiven for thinking, but how does this highly generalised account of the evolution of post-war capitalism in the rich West translate into the real world, with its myriad complexity? It's high time we explored more fully some of those contextually specific pathways of neoliberalisation. Almost all states have embraced, sometimes voluntarily and in other instances in response to coercive pressures, some version of neoliberal theory and adjusted at least some policies and practices accordingly (Harvey, 2007, p 3), but here we focus on developments in the 'heartland' of neoliberalism – the countries associated with Anglo-Saxon capitalism and its credit-financed, consumption-driven growth model. Accordingly, the next section presents two mini-case studies of real-world variation within this grouping of finance-led economies. The first explores the return of the super-rich, and the second, Canada's seeming immunity from the global banking crisis.

First, however, we need to flesh out the varieties of capitalist democracy referred to in the Introduction earlier. Let's start with the Anglo-Saxon variant, as practised in the English-speaking world (the US, UK, Canada, Ireland, Australia and New Zealand). Stereotypically, Anglo-Saxon capitalism is characterised by lower taxes, less government regulation and greater ease for firms to hire and fire employees – and also to take each other over through mergers and acquisitions. At the level of individual firms and businesses, it emphasises shareholder value maximisation as a core principle of corporate governance, which implies that the ultimate measure of a company's success in rewarding shareholders is the short-term performance of its share price.

Anglo-Saxon capitalism is often contrasted with the 'social market economy' of Rhenish or Rhineland capitalism – also known as the German model – and with Asian, especially Japanese, versions of capitalism. The Japanese model, and Asian capitalism in general, has traditionally shared the social market economy's emphasis on long-term relationships with 'stakeholders' other than shareholders, especially employees and 'house' banks that provide what is termed 'patient' capital to non-financial companies, either by virtue of a significant long-term ownership stake in the company, or through making long-term loans. The Japanese variant is, however, more accepting of the idea of a state-led industrial policy (see ft.com/lexicon on Anglo-Saxon capitalism). Another variant is 'Nordic capitalism', where firms operate against the background of a high-tax, high-spend government.

Sometimes the Rhenish and Nordic countries of continental Europe are described as 'coordinated market economies' in opposition to the 'liberal market economies' of the Anglo-Saxon world, with their more competitive market mechanisms for the governance of company relations (Hall and Soskice, 2001).

We can also identify a Southern European or 'Club Med' variety of capitalism, in countries (Spain, Italy, Greece and Portugal) with fragmented trade unions and employers with limited capacity to coordinate labour market outcomes, whose economies have traditionally generated economic and employment growth through high levels of domestic consumption. These countries have weak welfare states and a significant amount of social welfare occurs through family relations (Regan, 2013). Their party political systems are often portrayed as being 'clientelistic' or dominated by patron–client relationships, where the patron (the party organisation) offers selective benefits such as help in the labour market (especially access to public sector jobs) or favouritism in administrative decisions (exemption from military service, the granting of building permits, and so on) to the 'client' (sometimes the least privileged members of the community) in exchange for votes (Hopkin, 2015).

Real-world variation of the sort sketched above is historically grounded and shaped by nationally specific institutional contexts. Neoliberalism does not emerge fully formed, and is best thought of as a political project whose success requires that it be embedded within countries exemplifying a variety of models of capitalism, some of which will be more receptive to neoliberalism than others. In reality, such a project, although it may be presumed to reflect the ideological preferences of policy-makers, is 'path dependent' in the sense that it must be implemented through a structure of political and administrative institutions inherited from the past. 'Historical institutionalism', as this approach is known in political science, implies a course of evolution rather than a complete following of the path: there will be change and development, but the range of possibilities will have been constrained by the formative period of the institution or policy (Peters, 1999, pp 62-5).

For example, in a number of continental European countries such as Germany and Sweden there is a tradition of a tripartite 'social contract' between employers, trade unions and government to work together to reach coordinated policies on wages, prices, taxation and social benefits. Consequently, collective bargaining and employment rights are strongly entrenched in such countries, notwithstanding pressure to deregulate employment conditions. This corporate approach,[1] which is not to be confused with the corporate governance of business firms, although it encompasses this domain, is reinforced in welfare states of Bismarckian origin, where insurance-based contributions – especially those levied on employers – finance a much larger proportion of welfare spending than in the UK, and where trade unions and employers are directly involved in managing the various social insurance funds.[2]

Institutions also embed interests: as Pierson (1994) demonstrated in connection with the retrenchment of the welfare state in the Reagan-Thatcher era, policies for change must also be sensitive to the politics of change. This is because existing institutions tend to 'lock in' the veto power of producer interests (welfare professionals such as teachers) and programme beneficiaries (welfare recipients) opposed to change. Realistically, then, we can expect any change programme to meet with resistance from beneficiaries of the status quo, and also to be uneven in its impact as between one state or jurisdiction and another.

The regulation approach, understood as an account of capitalist development in terms of a succession of relatively stable phases of capitalist growth punctuated by periodic crises, is unable to provide a complete explanation of the origins of specific policy measures and their implementation, or of the precise contours of a new state form, organisation of work, or evolving financial regime. To accommodate this complexity and real-world variation, regulationists need to enlist the help of concepts and explanations drawn from theoretical perspectives operating at a lower level of abstraction such as the historical institutionalist framework alluded to above, which holds that institutions broadly defined – those that establish the rules of the game for political struggles (Pierson, 1996, p 152) – make a real difference to policy choices and outcomes.

This means that a country's constitutional arrangements, pattern of party politics, administrative traditions and style of corporate governance all matter. So, too, do sets of beliefs or 'ruling ideas', which lock policy-makers into often inappropriate policy responses. And so, too, as the first case study demonstrates, does 'policy drift' – systematic, prolonged failures of government to respond to the shifting realities of a dynamic economy (Hacker and Pierson, 2011, p 43).

The return of the super-rich

It has not gone unnoticed that one of the most striking parallels between the financial crash of 2008 and the Great Depression of 1929, both of which originated in the US, is that the years running up to both crises – the early 2000s and the 1920s – witnessed the development of very high levels of income and wealth inequality as financial activities boomed (Martin et al, 2014, p 5). No less clear is that the impact of the most recent wave of financialisation on the distribution of income and wealth in the rich, capitalist democracies of the world has been markedly greater in some countries, the UK and above all, the US, than in others. The runaway pay and bonuses of Wall Street and City of London bankers is our cue to look more closely at the trajectory of rising inequality in the two countries at the leading edge of financialisation.

Growing extremes of income and wealth should worry us all. This is not just because the relentless search by the rich and super-rich for high returns on their investments feeds the growth of speculative financial activity, leading in turn to stock and real estate bubbles. Or because the growing gap between the snowballing pay of top earners and the stagnating or declining pay of lower and middle-income households means that ordinary people have come to rely more and more on debt, especially mortgage debt, to maintain their lifestyles. We should also be concerned because there is plenty of evidence to suggest that growing disparities in income, wealth and life chances are associated with a rise in the incidence of socio-medical pathologies such as depression, alcoholism and obesity (Wilkinson and Pickett, 2009). Not least, we should all be concerned that rising inequality is eroding the 'social compact' that holds market economies and societies together.

Defining and measuring inequalities of income and wealth is itself a complex task, and a great deal of academic firepower has been, and continues to be, devoted to separating out the myths from the facts. Reaching definitive conclusions about how unequal a society really is needs high-quality information from national representative surveys, of the sort gathered by government departments, by official statistical agencies such as the UK's Office for National Statistics (ONS), and by universities and other independent research institutions. Likewise, there are many different ways of comparing how unequal countries are, depending on what kind of inequality is of most concern – between those at the bottom and those in the middle of an income distribution, between those near the top and those near the bottom, or between the very poorest and the very richest (Hills, 2015, pp 24-6).

It is also important to be aware of the distinction between 'income' – a *flow* of money (like pay) that people receive each week, month or year – and 'wealth' – the market value of the accumulated *stock* of assets that people own, such as their savings or, if they are lucky, their home, minus any debts. While the data on assets is of lower quality than the data on income, it seems clear that inequality of wealth has grown nearly everywhere over the past 30 years, and also that the distribution of wealth is more unequal than the distribution of income – due, at least in part, to its accumulation through inheritances and to appreciation in the market value of wealthy people's assets (Allaire and Firsirotu, 2014, p 16; Sayer, 2015, pp 10, 97). To fully understand the phenomenon of economic and social inequality, it is also necessary to take into consideration unequal intergenerational social mobility as well as inter-regional variations in the distribution of income and wealth within a country, such as the infamous north–south divide in countries such as the UK and Italy.

One very useful source of information on the distribution of household income in the Anglo-Saxon world is the World Top Incomes database managed by Facundo Alvaredo, Tony Atkinson, Emmanuel Saez and Thomas Piketty, which uses official tax data. This database makes available historical data relating to Australia, Canada, Ireland, New Zealand, the UK and US (the countries of Atlantic Fordism), as well as a number of other countries in Europe and Asia. Using the tax year 2009-10 (referred to as 2009 in the database) – the most recent year for which figures for Ireland are available – as the base year, my search of the database reveals that the *pre-tax* or gross income share of the top 1 per cent of households in that year was 8.88 per cent in Australia, 12.29 per cent in Canada, 10.50 per cent in Ireland, 7.84 per cent in New Zealand, 15.42 per cent in the UK and 16.68 per cent in the US (figures retrieved from Alvaredo et al on 14 August 2015). The UK figure must, however, be interpreted in the context of the bringing forward of income in advance of the introduction of a 50 per cent rate of tax on top income earners (Atkinson, 2013).

Table 1, which compares the distribution of top incomes in the two most unequal countries in the group – the UK and US – from 2009 through to 2012 (the latest available year for the UK) reveals something that the 2009 'snapshot' cannot: a growing gap between the two countries in the income share going to the top 1 per cent, and particularly the top 0.1 per cent or one out of every thousand households.

Table 1: Share of pre-tax income obtained by the top 1 per cent and 0.1 per cent income groups in the UK and US (2009-2012)

	Top 1% income share UK	Top 0.1% income share UK	Top 1% income share US	Top 0.1% income share US
2009	15.42%	6.40%	16.68%	7.04%
2010	12.55%	4.66%	17.45%	7.52%
2011	12.93%	4.80%	17.47%	7.38%
2012	12.70%	4.60%	18.88%	8.36%

There are, of course, shortcomings with using tax statistics. Rich people, in particular, have a strong incentive to under-report their taxable incomes and to present their returns in a way that reduces tax liability. They also make use of tax havens that allow income to be moved beyond the reach of national tax authorities. But tax records are still the best 'DNA evidence' available, much better than survey results in capturing the distribution of economic rewards (Hacker and Pierson, 2011, pp 14-15).

But there are many other sources of income data. For example, using official Department for Work and Pensions (DWP) figures for the distribution of *disposable* income in the UK (after benefits and direct taxes, and adjusted for household size), John Hills, Professor of Social Policy at the London School of Economics and Political Science (LSE), has demonstrated a slow decline in the share of income going to the middle fifth quintile of the income distribution, the famously squeezed 'middle Britain'. Back in 1979 these households received 18 per cent of total income, but this fell to 17 per cent in 1996-97 and again to 16 per cent in 2010-11. Contrary to a widely held myth, this was not because the squeezed middle was losing ground to the poorest fifth, whose share of income fell from 10 per cent in 1979 to level out at 8 per cent in both 1996-97 and 2010-11. Instead, the explanation for the declining share of the *bottom four-fifths* of UK households over this period is that the share of the top fifth grew from 35 per cent in 1979 to 41 per cent in 1996-97, and 42 per cent in 2010-11. In fact, virtually all of this increase in both the Conservative and Labour years went to the top 10 per cent, up from 21 to 26 per cent of the total, with little change for the next-to-top tenth (Hills, 2015, pp 42-3).

Hills has also made use of the World Top Incomes database to show that most of the UK increase accruing to the top 10 per cent actually went to the top 1 per cent, whose *after-tax* income share doubled from 4.7 per cent of the national total in 1979 to 9.5 per cent in 1996 and 12.6 per cent on the eve of the credit crunch in 2007 (Hills, 2015, pp 43-4, citing figures downloaded from Alvaredo et al on 15 April 2014).[3]

Let's move on to the US, and particularly to the role played by Washington (the US federal government) in making the rich richer since the 1980s. Basing their calculations on tax data and income surveys gathered by the Congressional Budget Office (Congress' nonpartisan budget agency), two of America's most distinguished political scientists have concluded that the gap between the rich, especially the super-rich, and those left behind by the advancing tide of the 'winner-take-all economy' is much greater now than a generation ago, and has no real parallel elsewhere in the capitalist democracies of the world (Hacker and Pierson, 2011, pp 38-9). Jacob Hacker and Paul Pierson found that in the period from 1979 to 2006 the average inflation-adjusted *after-tax* income (from all sources, including wages, salaries, self-employment income, retirement pensions, transfer and in-kind benefits, plus dividends, capital gains, interest and rent) of the poorest 20 per cent of US households rose from US$14,900 to US$16,500, a meagre 10 per cent gain over 27 years. The middle quintile of households did better, but not much better. Their average after-tax income rose from US$42,900 to US$52,100, a gain of 21 per cent or just 0.7 per cent a year.

By contrast, the average after-tax income of the richest 1 per cent of households rose from US$337,000 a year in 1979 to more than US$1.2 million in 2006, an increase of nearly 260 per cent. Even so, the incomes of the top 1 per cent pale in comparison to those received by the top 0.1 per cent (comprising, for the most part, corporate executives, investment bankers and hedge fund managers and their families, not sports stars and celebrities). Between 1979 and 2005, their average income increased from just over US$4 million to nearly US$24.3 million (Hacker and Pierson, 2011, pp 22-4).

These statistics tell a stark story: while the income of most US households has stagnated (and this despite women being much more likely to be part of the workforce than a generation ago, augmenting both family income and the number of hours worked by household members), most of the income growth has gone to the very richest Americans. In 2007 the pay of the average chief executive officer of a large US corporation was accelerating towards 300 times the earnings of the typical worker, compared with around 24 times typical earnings in 1965. Not only are American bosses paid more than their counterparts in other rich nations, a huge chunk of their pay is hidden in deferred compensation – pay that is put off to defer taxes on interest and earnings – and in guaranteed-benefit pensions (Hacker and Pierson, 2011, p 64).

The US itself did not look all that exceptional in the early 1970s. A generation ago, France, Germany, Switzerland and Canada all had a higher share of national income going to the top 1 per cent. But that has all changed: while the aforementioned countries experienced little or no increase in the share of income going to such households in the period from the mid-1970s to about 2000, the share going to the top 1 per cent of US households more or less doubled, from 8 to 16 per cent.

It is true that other English-speaking countries, particularly Canada and the UK, have followed a path more like that of the US. There is almost certainly a 'contagion' effect at work here, as companies in both these countries have faced intense competitive pressure to match the salaries on offer in the US. In the UK, FTSE 100 chief executives now typically earn 120 times as much as their average employee, up from 47 times as much in 2000 (as reported in *The Economist*, 25 October, 2014). Tellingly, however, there is little sign of the same meteoric rise in top salaries in French-speaking Québec (Hacker and Pierson, 2011, p 40).[4]

This undoubtedly owes something to the development in Québec in the 1960s of a francophone and statist political economy, whose distinctive features are traceable to a combination of Québec's Catholic past, French language and sense of being a small nation needing to compete in a continental, English-speaking market (Clark, 2004). In the 1990s, several Canadian provincial governments, notably Alberta and Ontario, warmly embraced the neoliberal agenda of slimming the (provincial) state, and attempted a downsizing that went far beyond what was needed to balance the provincial budget, but Québec was not one of them (Clark, 2002).

The Quiet Revolution, as it is called, produced a Québec growth model with recognisably neo-corporatist features, with a close intermingling of state and trade union power. This gave way to a 'new social economy' version of the Québec model in the mid-1990s, based on new forms of partnership between the state and voluntary and community-based organisations, although some commentators have suggested that, irrespective of the development of a new social economy at its periphery, the Québec state remained unreconstructedly neo-corporatist at its core (Clark, 2004).[5] Either way, this is not a growth model conducive to run-away executive pay packages.

In explaining how the US, 'winner-take-all' economy has come to be set apart from other rich nations, Hacker and Pierson reject what they see as the standard view that the massive redistribution of income has been caused by the shift towards more knowledge-based employment, or what is often referred to in the literature as skill-biased technological change (SBTC). The SBTC approach holds that markets determine the link between technological change and income distribution, with the skill-biased characteristics of that technology affecting the demand for labour with different types of skills. While not denying that technological shifts have played a part in determining the returns to different types of labour, Hacker and Pierson's position is that such technologically driven explanations have little to say about why the hyper-concentration of income at the very top has been more pronounced in the US than elsewhere. Instead, their explanation focuses on the politics of 'winner-take-all'. More precisely, financial and labour markets have been politically reconstructed to aid the privileged, and executive pay is set in a distorted market deeply shaped by public policy (Hacker and Pierson, 2011, pp 45, 62).

The reasons for the emergence of the winner-take-all economy include:

- The 'rollback' of taxation for those at the very top (and the favourable tax treatment of private equity and hedge fund managers that allows the fees paid to them by investors to be treated as capital gains rather than income).
- 'Policy drift' (the absence of any government response to rising inequality or to a system of corporate governance that allows chief executive officers to drive up their own stock-based pay).
- The shredding of the post-New Deal rulebook for financial markets.

- The decline of US trade unions, whose membership fell from nearly a quarter of the private sector workforce in the early 1970s to just over 7 per cent in 2010. In the 1960s, the rates of unionisation in Canada and the US were very similar, at about one-third of wage and salary workers, but the gap has opened dramatically over the past four decades, over which time trade union membership in Canada has seen relatively little decline. Hacker and Pierson attribute the gap to the much lower (and declining) likelihood in the US that workers who have an interest in joining a union – broadly the same percentage in both countries – will actually belong to one, as a result of aggressive anti-union activities by employers that have met with little resistance from public authorities (Hacker and Pierson, 2011, p 60).

Their central point bears repeating: the 'winner-take-all' economy did not happen because international markets, or globalisation, or differentials in education or life chances made it inevitable, but because politicians and public officials allowed it to happen. More often than not, it was due to policy drift: the politicians were persuaded to do nothing, to let up on enforcement, to give in to the pressure of the financial lobbyists.

There are striking parallels here with how the UK built a new, post-colonial overseas empire from the 1960s in the form of a 'spider's web' of offshore tax havens or secrecy jurisdictions, with the City of London at its heart. Admittedly, this was a deliberately constructed counterpart to the eurodollar markets, which grew under their own internal logic, but as the spider's web spread in waves from the Crown dependencies near the British mainland (the Channel Islands and the Isle of Man) to British-held territories overseas, so each new offshore centre would put competitive pressure on the tax, legal and regulatory systems of the jurisdictions nearby, forcing the pace of their financial liberalisation whether they liked it or not (Shaxson, 2012, p 104). The archives, says Shaxson, tell a consistent story about how the tax havens grew: 'private sector operators working in a zone of extreme freedom began to call the shots, with little opposition from Britain' (Shaxson, 2012, p 106).

These days, many of the world's most successful tax havens are former or current British imperial outposts, and the relationship with the mother country reassures the super-rich and the financial services industry that the UK will step in if needs be to protect the tax haven from external attacks (Runciman, 2011).

Let's note, too, that Hacker and Pierson's argument that Washington is to blame for the emergence of the 'winner-take-all' economy has not gone unchallenged. Bill Lazonick provides an alternative explanation rooted in the financialisation of the US corporation. Yes, 'value extraction' is partly the result of political lobbying for deregulation and lower tax rates, but in a paper co-authored with Mariana Mazzucato (2012), Lazonick argues that it also occurs because top corporate executives and large institutional shareholders are able to use their positional power to reap a return on their investment that is disproportionate to the risk they assume, while workers and taxpayers (who make a significant contribution to the innovation process by funding the leading role played by the US government in technology development) extract much less value than they create. A large chunk of the enormous incomes of top executives in US corporations has come from gains obtained from cashing in stock options awarded them by their boards of directors. As well as reducing incentives to invest in innovation and denying US workers employment opportunities, stock-based executive remuneration has been a major cause of the increasing inequality of income in the US (Lazonick and Mazzucato, 2012; see also Lazonick, 2013, pp 871-9).

Why was Canada exempt from the crash?

Canada is interesting for another reason, too. The federal government has resisted many of the efforts of financial interests to rewrite the rules of the financial game, and Canada has been largely spared the financial debacle of the past few years (Hacker and Pierson, 2011, p 68).[6] No Canadian financial institutions failed in 2008. Again, it is historical institutional factors that best explain these divergent outcomes. The US has one of the world's more fragmented and diversified financial systems, with almost 7,000 chartered banks and a legion of regulators, reflecting its origins in local community-based banking. Historically, most US states have had some form of restrictions on 'branching' (acquisitions by large, national banks of smaller, local banks) across state lines, and within states in some cases. The result has been that there are a lot of US banks. At the peak almost 100 years ago, there were 31,000 individual institutions, virtually one distinct bank for every city and town, and almost no branches (Haltom, 2014, p 22).

The Canadian financial system, by contrast, is much more concentrated. Canada has just 80 banks, six of which hold 93 per cent of the market share. It has one overarching financial regulator, the Office of the Superintendent of Financial Institutions (OSFI), which oversees all financial institutions: banks, mortgage lenders, insurance companies, pension funds, and so on (securities markets are regulated by Canada's 13 provincial and territorial governments, but their regulations are largely harmonised). When OSFI was established in 1987, it encompassed most financial activity, including off balance sheet activities that occur outside of the banking sector in the US. Nowhere do these structural and regulatory differences manifest themselves more clearly than in mortgage finance. Canadian banks tend to hold on to mortgages rather than sell them to investors. Fewer than a third of Canadian mortgages were securitised before the financial crisis, compared to almost two-thirds of mortgages in the US. Fewer than 3 per cent of Canadian mortgages were classified as sub-prime before the crisis, compared with 15 per cent in the US (Haltom, 2014, p 25).

But Canada's financial system was largely unsupervised until the late 1980s. In a period in which both Canada and the US had virtually no official supervision or regulation of bank risk-taking – from the 1830s to the advent of the Fed in 1913 – the US experienced no fewer than 10 systemic banking crises, while Canada had only two brief and mild credit crunches during the same period, neither of which involved significant bank failures (Calomiris and Haber, 2014, p 5). That suggests that regulation alone can't explain Canada's financial stability. Arguably the fact that its system includes only a relatively small number of players means that mutual monitoring by banks in exchange for the implied promise of mutual support in crises is more feasible in Canada. This, combined with tight regulatory standards, gives Canadian banks a stronger incentive to avoid excessive risk-taking and to make mortgages safe (Haltom, 2014, p 22).[7]

Both mini-case studies – and also the Australian experience alluded to a moment ago – testify to the complex ways in which political forces, historically embedded traditions and existing organisational arrangements produce different pathways of neoliberalisation even within the same group of countries that make up its heartland. They also demonstrate that however useful historical institutional research can be in enabling more fine-grained, cross-national analysis of 'real regulation', it cannot always provide definitive explanations of policy outcomes and/or of the actual mechanism of policy or institutional change – witness the different positions adopted by Lazonick and Mazzucato, on the one hand, and Hacker and Pierson, on the other, as to whether it is value extraction in business organisations or the politics of winner-take-all that is the prime driver of the increase in inequality over the last three decades.[8] This is no less true of Charles Calomiris and Stephen Haber's cross-national study, referenced above, of the historical evolution of banking systems.

In explaining why the US banking system is highly crisis-prone while others, notably Canada, have experienced few or no systemic banking crises, Calomiris and Haber place great store on the structure of a country's political institutions and in particular, on the nature of the political coalition that gets to determine the rules of the banking game, including who can and cannot access credit. As we have seen in the US, because of its federal structure, banking policy ended up largely in the hands of the states. As a consequence, it was political elites at the state level, typically small-town merchants and farmers, who came to dominate. The result, for most of American history, was a fragmented system of tiny banks that were highly vulnerable to local downturns and subject to frequent panics. By contrast, in Canada, primarily because colonial Britain wanted to limit the autonomy of French Canada, banking policy was centralised in the national government, and Canada ended up with a small number of large banks with an extensive and diversified network of nationwide branches, which proved to be more resilient in hard times.

In the US case, the nub of Calomiris and Haber's argument is that the original political coalition between independent 'unit' banks providing financial services to their local communities and small farmers came to be replaced by a new coalition between the rapidly growing commercial mega-banks and politicians representing urban activist groups – a coalition forged, among other things, by the commitment of the commercial banks to channel vast amounts of credit through activist groups in exchange for the political support of those groups for bank mergers between 1992 and 2007.

Many steps were required to make these arrangements work, but one of the most crucial was that 'Fannie Mae' and 'Freddie Mac' were pressured by the Clinton administration to lower their underwriting standards dramatically so that loans to urban working-class households could become part of Fannie and Freddie's portfolios. Once they agreed to do so, their progressively weaker underwriting standards applied to *everyone*: the politics of regulatory approval for bank mergers set in motion a process whose ultimate outcome was that large swathes of the American middle class were able to take advantage of mortgage underwriting rules that, compared to those of other countries and of earlier periods of America's own history, were inconceivably lax (Calomiris and Haber, 2014, p 19).

Although certainly part of the story behind the rise of sub-prime lending, this is a partial and controversial explanation that is at odds with the findings of the Financial Crisis Inquiry Commission that Fannie and Freddie followed rather than led Wall Street and other lenders in the rush for fool's gold (see Chapter Two). Likewise, it fails to explain why so much sub-prime lending was done by financial institutions other than commercial banks – by investment banks, by hedge funds and by the new breed of mortgage lenders with poor underwriting standards like Countrywide Financial, which in 2006 financed 20 per cent of all mortgages in the US – or why such a large percentage of the mortgage securities ended up in the hands of foreign banks, none of which were subject to the same US federal government pressure (Ahamed, 2014).

Notes

[1] 'Corporatism' has its origins in 19th-century Roman Catholic social thought, and refers to a form of organisation in which the economy remains capitalist in the sense of being privately owned, but the stability of the overall capitalist system is ensured through the close relationship between political and economic arrangements and a moral order based on Catholic doctrine. In its contemporary usage in Western democracies, corporatism refers to a system of economic tripartism involving negotiations between the government and interest groups representing capital and labour to establish economic policy. The organisations that represent workers (and business) in the system are also expected to ensure voluntary compliance with the agreed policy outcomes, especially wage moderation. This is sometimes also referred to as 'neo-corporatism' (Crouch, 1982, pp 145-6).

[2] Otto von Bismarck (1815-96), the first Chancellor of united Germany, was a Conservative politician and 'reluctant collectivist' who pioneered a system of collective welfare based on social insurance principles. The programme, as implemented between 1884 and 1889, was designed to appease the working class and weaken support for socialism. It included health, accident (workman's compensation) and disability insurance, and an old-age retirement pension. Traditionally, the Bismarckian model has focused on generous employment-based rights, but with weaker rights for those outside the labour market. Benefit entitlements are based on occupational groupings, while rates of payment for periods of economic inactivity including retirement are in proportion to earnings. The capacity of the Bismarckian model to adapt to the challenges of neoliberal globalisation, social and demographic change, intensified European integration, and now, post-crash austerity has received considerable attention in a growing academic literature on the future of the European welfare state. One recent, authoritative study of the Bismarckian welfare regime type – which includes the six founding EU member states of Germany, France, Italy and the Benelux countries, along with Spain and Austria as well as the Czech Republic, Slovakia, Hungary and Poland – concluded that successive rounds of retrenchment and 'path-breaking' structural reform have reinforced the division between insured insiders and assisted and/or 'activated' outsiders (assisted, that is, by means-tested, taxpayer-funded benefits and activated into employment by 'atypical' labour contracts that deliver insecure jobs

and social protection) in what have become effectively 'dual labour market, dual welfare' systems (Palier, 2010, pp 383-5). That said, there is no real consensus in the literature as to whether the different types of European welfare state are moving closer together, in the sense that, notwithstanding persisting institutional differences between them, they are delivering similar policy outcomes.

[3] Readers wishing to familiarise themselves with the distribution of *wealth* in the UK are recommended to consult the information and analysis produced by two independent research organisations: the Institute for Fiscal Studies (see, for example, Crossley and O'Dea, 2010) and the University of Birmingham's Commission on the Distribution of Wealth (see, for example, Rowlingson, 2012), as well as the overview in Part 1 of Martin et al (2014). For more extended analysis and discussion of the latest research findings concerning inequality and the top 1 per cent in the UK, see Dorling (2014). There are a number of other UK-based organisations with a reputation for producing high-quality research reports on poverty and poverty-related themes (wages, incomes and living standards, social security and housing policy, and so on). These include the Joseph Rowntree Foundation (jrf.org. uk), the Resolution Foundation (resolutionfoundation.org) and the Centre for the Analysis of Social Exclusion at LSE (sticed.lse.uk/case).

[4] On the disparity at the top of the income pyramid (*after* taxes and income transfers) in Canada and Québec as compared to the US, see Allaire and Firsirotu (2014). Their overall conclusion is that despite the strong increase in the remuneration of Canadian executives from 2006, Canada and Québec still stand apart, with their more moderate level of inequality of wealth and their greater social mobility, from the US. In 2010, the total income share captured by the top 1 per cent in the US (14.9 per cent) was more than twice that of the top 1 per cent in Québec (7.2 per cent). If one considers the distribution of gross income more finely by adding capital gains, here again Québec is clearly different from the rest of Canada and very strongly different from the US. In 2011, the group representing the top 0.1 per cent of incomes captured only 3.7 per cent of total income in Québec, compared to 4.9 per cent in Canada and 9.3 per cent in the US. The corresponding figures for the 1 per cent group are 11.5 per cent in Québec, 13.2 per cent in Canada and 19.7 per cent in the US.

It should also be noted that the income threshold for inclusion in the 1 per cent and 0.1 per cent groups in Canada varies by province. Thus, in 2011, a net income of $133,300 was sufficient to join the top 1 per cent in Québec, while the income threshold for the same group was $229,400 in Alberta and $169,400 in Ontario (figures cited are Canadian dollars). For the top 0.1 per cent group the difference in the threshold is even greater:

$416,200 in Québec compared to $933,500 in Alberta and $617,100 in Ontario (Allaire and Firsirotu, 2014, pp 9-10). Income statistics for Québec based on the language of the form used for the tax return indicate that the growth in the share of total income earned by the top 1 per cent and 0.1 per cent groups is much lower among Francophones than Anglophones (Veall, 2012).

[5] The 'social economy' as defined by Amin et al (2002, p vii) consists of 'non-profit activities designed to combat social exclusion through socially useful goods sold in the market (and) which are not provided for by the state or the private sector'. The concept dates back to the 19th century, when various novel types of non-state, non-market organisations such as cooperative and friendly societies and other (social) enterprises aimed at organising production, consumption and access to credit, healthcare and other services on a mutual or self-help basis, were founded.

[6] So, too, has Australia. Stephen Bell and Andrew Hindmoor, in their comparative study of banking and financial systems in the US, UK, Canada and Australia, also adopt a historical institutional approach to explain why the US and UK systems imploded but the Canadian and Australian ones did not. They conclude that banking crises, or their absence, are largely driven by the nature of the banking markets found in individual countries. Thus, banks in Australia and Canada could make good profits through traditional lending practices, and did not face the same incentives to outperform the market that were present within the more deregulated, competitive financial systems of the US and UK. But their analysis also highlights the importance of bank-centric institutional factors, particularly differences in senior bankers' beliefs, in explaining why not all bankers succumbed to the lure of highly leveraged trading even in the financial heartlands of the US and the UK (Bell and Hindmoor, 2015, p 333).

[7] The investigative journalist Bruce Livesey (2013) provides a much less flattering view of the performance of the Canadian financial sector: that beneath the veneer of stability it was a haven for securities fraud. According to Livesey, although no Canadian bank became insolvent during the financial crisis, securities regulation by the provincial authorities was largely ineffectual, and the federal government was obliged to intervene to move tens of billions of dollars in assets off the banks' balance sheets to enable them to continue lending.

Walks and Clifford (2015) argue that it was the willingness and ability of the Canadian federal government to control and make use of the process of mortgage securitisation, not prudent banking, that enabled Canada to emerge relatively unscathed through the crisis – and that, seven years on, has turned the Canadian housing market into one of the most expensive in the world.

[8] SBTC sees the negative impact of technological change on the demand for unskilled (generally non-college educated) relative to skilled (generally college-educated) workers in the labour market as the main driver of inequality (Lazonick and Mazzucato, 2012, p 20).

FIVE

Post-crash austerity

The policy of reducing Germany to servitude for a generation, of degrading the lives of millions of human beings, and of depriving a whole nation of happiness should be abhorrent and detestable – abhorrent and detestable, even if it were possible, even if it enriched ourselves, even if it did not sow the decay of the whole civilised life of Europe. (Keynes, 1920)

Let's remind ourselves of the scope and scale of the crash and its aftermath. In the words of the report of the National Commission set up to inquire into the causes of the financial and economic crisis in the US:

While the vulnerabilities that created the potential for crisis were years in the making, it was the collapse of the housing bubble – fuelled by low interest rates, easy and available credit, scant regulation, and toxic mortgages – that was the spark that ignited a string of events, which led to a full-blown crisis in the fall of 2008. Trillions of dollars in risky mortgages had become embedded throughout the financial system, as mortgage-related securities were packaged, repackaged, and sold to investors around the world. When the bubble burst, hundreds of billions of dollars in losses in mortgages and mortgage-related securities shook markets as well as financial institutions that had significant exposures to those mortgages and had borrowed heavily against them. This happened not just in the United States but around the world. (Financial Crisis Inquiry Commission, 2011, p xvi)

In the aftermath of the crash, national taxpayers were forced to bail out irresponsible banks to the tune of trillions of dollars, and Western governments to make deep cuts in the welfare state in order to satisfy the anxieties of the financial markets over the size of the public debt – those self-same 'bond vigilantes'[1] who fuelled asset bubbles and, in the case of the 'too big to fail' banks, whose rescue contributed so significantly to the debt in the first place.

The road to austerity

In the UK, the policy response to the financial crash and ensuing slump has been to seek to restore business confidence by engaging resolutely in what Paul Krugman (2012, p 200) has called 'unforced' austerity measures, with the Conservative-Liberal Democrat coalition government elected into office in May 2010 continuing to follow the neoliberal, market-led growth model pursued by its Labour predecessor, and holding strongly to the belief that reducing the public deficit would spark a private sector recovery.

Underlying immediate policy debates concerning the nature and timing of austerity policies, there was controversy over future growth strategies: should the government seek to restore the current model, basing growth on finance, retail, construction and private (and voluntary) sector delivery of public services, or should it pursue more direct measures to invest in public infrastructure and in small and medium-sized enterprises, the main source of innovation in the real economy (Taylor-Gooby, 2011)?

Following manifesto pledges to implement further public spending and welfare cuts and victory in the May 2015 general election, the new Conservative government led by David Cameron moved quickly to pursue its plans for continued austerity.[2] It is clear to many observers, myself included, that the Conservative administration regards austerity not simply as a means to get public spending under control, but as part of a longer-term project to shrink the state and, by extension, to create new markets for the 'public services industry' (see, for example, Crawford et al, 2015; TUC, 2015).[3]

There has been a lively debate among UK academic economists – virtually all of whom now accept that the deficit reduction policies pursued by the coalition government during its five years in power drew on a discredited theory of 'expansionary fiscal consolidation'[4] – over whether an anti-austerity policy would have been politically possible in 2010. Professor Simon Wren-Lewis of the University of Oxford has suggested that by raising value added tax (VAT) and cutting government spending – measures that could easily have been postponed until the recovery from recession was assured – the government delayed the recovery by three years. He considers that such a policy would have been possible had there been an appropriate professional consensus among macro-economists telling the politicians not to worry about the rising budget deficit (Wren-Lewis, 2015a).

In the event, a large group of UK economists, mainly those working in the City, were warning of an impending financial crisis if the fiscal deficit remained high. The media, always responsive to the views of financial market participants and fond of analogies between households and governments, successfully reinforced the 'common-sense' notion that the government should respond to a deficit by tightening its belt. Finally and crucially, Wren-Lewis suggests that the Greek debt crisis, which intensified during the course of 2010-12 (we'll come to that shortly), dealt a killer blow to the line that deficits could be safely ignored.

Austerity has been the only game in town in the Eurozone too, notwithstanding the ECB's belated (March 2015) launch of a major programme of quantitative easing (QE) designed to inject €1 trillion into the Eurozone economy by September 2016.[5] Eurozone countries have been forced to follow Germany's path to adjustment of the early to mid-2000s, by cutting government spending, reducing labour costs and selling more exports.

Whereas this policy combination allowed Germany to achieve a balanced budget and modest growth in the buoyant 2000s, imposing it across the board on the crisis-hit countries of the Eurozone has made for prolonged stagnation, with the accompanying social tension particularly pronounced in the debtor countries of the Southern and Western peripheries, the PIIGS. Continuing stagnation has led many economists to call for a more symmetrical adjustment of competitiveness, with Germany and other surplus countries shifting their domestic policies to increase public spending, wages and consumption at a faster rate. There have also been increasingly strident calls for structural reform of the Eurozone and for the extension of what is now a monetary union[6] into a banking and fiscal union, to enable conversion of the debts of the peripheral sovereigns into eurobonds for which the Eurozone member states would be jointly and severally liable (see, for example, Moravcsik, 2012; Wolf, 2014, pp 289-322; Legrain, 2015).

It has been a rather different story, at least until 2013, in the US. Here, despite the rhetoric of retrenchment, the Obama administration was able to pursue what Wyn Grant and Graham Wilson label a policy of 'inadvertent Keynesianism'. While US politicians continued to proclaim the virtues of deficit reduction and fiscal prudence, the increasingly deep divide between the Republican opposition (in favour of spending cuts as the exclusive means to achieve these goals) and the Democrats (who favoured tax increases as well, and resisted major spending cuts until the advent of the 2013 'sequester'[7]) resulted in the US maintaining a Keynesian-style fiscal stimulus, deficit spending approach. As a consequence, combined with the activism of the Fed in cutting interest rates and pursuing quantitative easing, the US emerged faster from the Great Recession than the countries practising austerity (Grant and Wilson, 2014, p viii).

Greece and the Eurozone

It would be tedious in the extreme to launch into a detailed description of the EU's institutional arrangements, and fortunately it is not necessary to do so to make sense of the Eurozone's sovereign debt crisis. But some background information is required, which I provide now, before resuming the narrative about the Greek debt crisis from where it was left off in Chapter Two.

It is helpful to think of the EU operating on two tracks, an intergovernmental track and a functional, 'everyday' track (McNamara, 2015). It is the intergovernmental track that has moved European integration forward over the years through a series of high-level negotiations involving national politicians sitting together as a *Council of Ministers*, the most important members of which are Germany's chancellor and France's president (and sometimes the UK's prime minister). These negotiations have moved the EU forwards from its Treaty of Rome (1958) beginnings as a common market via the Maastricht Treaty (1992), which created the euro,[8] to the Treaty of Lisbon (2007), which strengthened the EU's foreign policy presence. This is also the way in which the EU has expanded over time from its original six members to its current membership of 28 countries.

The second track is the low-level, 'integration by stealth' track associated with the European Commission based in Brussels. This is staffed by permanent officials, the so-called eurocrats, who work in partnership with national bureaucrats (civil servants) and business and other organisations to draft and oversee the implementation of the myriad rules and regulations – waste disposal regulations, water quality standards, and so on – that have an impact on the day-to-day lives of ordinary people in these 28 countries. There is also an 'emergency' track, labelled 'EU2' by Anthony Giddens (2014), which is where the real power lies when there are debt and other major crises. The leaders of France and Germany are normally key players in EU2, along with a finite and shifting number of other national politicians and sometimes the heads of international organisations (Giddens, 2014, p 6).[9]

There is one further, very significant, aspect of the institutional context left to comment on. This is the 'fiscal compact' (or Treaty on Stability, Coordination and Governance in the Economic and Monetary Union to give it its proper title), the successor to the Growth and Stability Pact, which came into force in January 2013 and is designed to enforce even stricter budgetary discipline on Eurozone countries. Member states were required for the first time to take legal, preferably constitutional, steps to impose national 'debt brakes' or 'golden rules' committing them to introduce balanced budgets and to keep their countries' debts from growing. The Treaty stipulates that the European Court of Justice, the judicial arm of the EU, will become the key enforcer of the compact, with the power to impose a fine of 0.1 per cent of GDP on countries that have not brought their deficit down within one year of ratification (Laskaridis, 2014, p 84). The aim of the fiscal compact is clear: to institutionalise fiscal 'consolidation' (reducing debt and deficits) indefinitely across Europe.

Greece received its first bailout loan in 2010, and has received two further loans since then, in 2012 and 2015. The first took place following mounting concern that Greece was about to default on its debts, with the EU countries and the IMF agreeing a €110 billion loan or 'rescue' package, including a bank recapitalisation worth €48 billion. This was the first of a number of sovereign debt crises in the Eurozone that have since come to be known collectively as the European sovereign debt crisis. In return, Greece was required to implement a major austerity and structural adjustment programme, which was approved by the Greek parliament in the context of widespread social unrest (Fazi, 2014, pp 39–40). In October 2011, the Troika offered a second bailout loan of €130 billion conditional on the imposition of further austerity and structural adjustment measures by the Greek government. The loan offer was originally rejected but, following the resignation of the government and the holding of new elections – and amid strong speculation that Greece would be forced to leave the Eurozone – the loan and its austerity conditions were approved by the new Greek parliament in 2012.

All private creditors holding Greek government bonds were required at the same time to sign a deal accepting extended maturities and a 53.5 per cent loss ('haircut') on the face value of what was owed them (Wikipedia, Greek government debt crisis).

The third bailout loan, worth €86 billion and spread over three years, was agreed in August 2015. As before, it was conditional on structural adjustment measures including labour market and pension reform and the sale of Greek state assets (to be administered by an independent trust fund), the proceeds of which are earmarked for the further recapitalisation of the Greek banks. The agreement included an additional €35 billion from EU funds to encourage job creation and growth in the Greek economy. The terms of the deal, which was negotiated under duress at a time when controls on cash withdrawals were in place in Greece due to the ECB's refusal to extend further emergency liquidity assistance to the country's insolvent banks, have been likened to the Versailles Treaty by the distinguished Harvard economist Amartya Sen (Sen, 2015).[10] The outcome of the deal was described by the German 'public intellectual' Jurgen Habermas as the 'de facto relegation of a member state to the status of a protectorate', and the privatisation fund as 'an act of punishment against a left-wing government'[11] (quoted in Oltermann, 2015).

Framing the Greek debt crisis

What you've just read is my attempt at an even-handed, factual account of the Greek debt crisis. Arguably, a deeper insight can be obtained by suggesting that the crisis can be understood or 'framed' in (at least) three different ways. I'm going to resist the temptation to over-specify these frames, which are deliberately provocative, as I think that if you've got this far in the book you'll be able to evaluate their usefulness without any further help from me. But let's begin by noting that unlike most accounts of the Great Recession, which see it as the consequence of a crisis brought about by profligate *lending*, accounts of the Greek (and wider Eurozone) debt crisis focus on profligate *borrowers*, private and public (Wren-Lewis, 2015c).

Frame 1

This framing of the Greek crisis focuses on the profligate borrowing of the Greek government, and more generally, on the notion that debtor states must at all times honour the claims of creditor states. Germany, however, is no ordinary creditor – not just because it is the largest creditor, but because it fears being encircled by a coalition of weak economies on the periphery of Europe. This fear of an anti-German coalition increased when in 2012 ECB President Mario Draghi promised to do 'whatever it takes' to save the euro, and announced a programme of Outright Monetary Transactions (OMT): unlimited outright purchases (initially from banks rather than directly from governments) of Spanish, Italian and other peripheral Eurozone country sovereign bonds, aimed at tackling speculation and stabilising interest rates. In most of Europe, the OMT initiative was seen as a breakthrough that saved the euro, but in Germany it was seen as a defeat – 'the night Merkel lost' (Kundnani, 2015).

Why so? Well, partly because Chancellor Merkel had famously commented shortly after the fall of Lehman Brothers in 2008, at a Party convention held in Stuttgart in Swabia (the most prosperous region of Germany and famous for the thriftiness of its people) that 'as the Swabian housewife knows', nobody (and by extension no country) can live beyond their means forever. And just as the Swabian housewife is the embodiment of economic virtue, so the debtor or 'fiscal sinner' lacks the necessary self-control to live within their means. This combination of the 'housewife' and the 'guilt' frame[12] of budgetary policy is key to understanding the Troika policy of bailouts-cum-austerity, which is rooted in a deeply engrained belief that debt relief or debt mutualisation through eurobonds would lead the debtor to engage in 'moral hazard' behaviour, thus further exploiting the creditor (Offe, 2015, pp 96-7).

This frame, then, may help to explain why German Finance Minister Wolfgang Schäuble has taken such an inflexible approach in the Greek bailout negotiations, and why Germany (and Austria) is so insistent on a 'debt brake' (*schuldenbremse*) being written into EU countries' constitutions.

Frame 2

This frame holds that the Greek debt crisis is not really about Greece at all, but is the continuation of a series of bailouts for German and French banks that lent irresponsibly to the governments of peripheral

Eurozone countries in the years preceding the great financial crash.[13] We've met this frame before in Chapter Two, where we encountered Mark Blyth's argument that the Eurozone crisis is really a banking, not a sovereign debt, crisis. The bailout loans were a means of shifting the liabilities of the banks onto the governments of the Eurozone as a whole. The implication of this frame (rescuing lenders by bailing out debtors) is that the Troika has deliberately ruled out debt forgiveness or extending debt maturities as an alternative policy option for resolving the crisis as this would mean that over-leveraged 'core' banks would have to pay at least some of the price for their excessive lending (Fazi, 2014, pp 83-4).

According to this frame, then, the first two bailout loans forced on Greece were, for the most part, used not to recapitalise Greek banks or rescue the Greek people, but to bail out German and French banks heavily exposed to Greek and other peripheral countries' sovereign bonds.[14] Although portrayed domestically as acts of sacrifice to save the periphery countries from the consequences of their own 'fecklessness', the German government's handling of the Greek/Eurozone debt crisis was first and foremost an opportunity to successfully 'Europeanise' or pass on to EU taxpayers much of the risk sitting on German banks' balance sheets (Thompson, 2013).

Frame 3

This frame proposes that the causes of the Greek debt crisis lie in Greek politics (Pappos, 2010). Whereas in the other PIIGS (Ireland and Spain in particular) the crisis was caused by excessive private borrowing encouraged by low interest rates following the adoption of the euro, Greece is the only country where there was an authentic fiscal or sovereign debt crisis from the outset. Greece's deficits and debts are symptoms, not causes, of the underlying problem – which is a combination of Greece's clientelistic political culture, the profligacy of successive Greek governments and the unwillingness or inability of the Greek state to collect taxes.[15]

According to this frame, Greece's clientelistic political parties were opposed to fiscal austerity because their own electoral survival depended on control of public sector jobs and budgets in order to reward 'clients'. It follows that recovery will require much more than wise economic management: solving the ongoing debt crisis will entail the remaking of Greece's whole political and institutional system.[16]

Whatever its causes, 'moving on' from the Greek debt crisis is going to be a fraught and difficult enterprise. It is not just that the actually existing monetary union, with its entrenched austerity rules, is not working in the way anticipated by mainstream economic theory (O'Rourke, 2015). Even the IMF has stated that Greece's debt can now only be made sustainable through debt relief measures that go far beyond what Europe has been willing to consider so far (IMF, 2015). The way the crisis has been handled has significantly deepened political divisions between the Club Med and Northern European countries, and the relationship between France and Germany has also been severely damaged. Greece remains mired in a slump of Great Depression proportions, and the brushing aside of the results of its referendum has been described as 'an attack on Greek democracy' (Stiglitz, 2015).

It is clear that what is at stake is much more than the stalling of an economic project. Let's leave the last (sobering) word to the German academic Claus Offe, who describes the Greek crisis as 'the cumulative outcome of a *financial market* crisis, a *sovereign debt* crisis, an *economic/ employment* crisis and an *institutional* crisis of the EU, its Eurozone and its democratic qualities' (Offe, 2015, p 1 emphasis in the original). Indeed, with the EU's institutional machinery incapable of resolving issues of redistribution and conflicting claims on resources, and key areas of decision-making insulated from democratic contestation, 'we are not only in a crisis – we are… in a *trap* where…movement is incapacitated (and) escape routes blocked' (Offe, 2015, p 3).

Notes

[1] In the bond market, you'll remember, prices move inversely to yields. Bond vigilantes are market investors who, when they perceive that inflation or credit risk is rising, sell bonds, thus increasing yields. The term signifies the ability of the bond market to serve as a restraint on a government's ability to over-spend and over-borrow (Wikipedia, Bond vigilante).

[2] Focusing on the economic dimension of austerity, as I do in this section, obscures the social, emotional and financial impact of budget cuts and welfare restructuring on the unemployed, on people with low-paid or insecure jobs, on single mothers and on those dependent on social benefits. For a useful corrective, see Clark and Heath (2015) and also Wilcox (2014), a study by the Joseph Rowntree Foundation of the impact on disabled residents of the UK coalition government's 'bedroom tax', which reduces the amount of housing benefit that council and housing association tenants can claim if they have spare bedrooms.

[3] Crawford et al comment that Conservative election manifesto pledges to provide 30 hours per week of free childcare to all three- and four year-olds with working parents, and to protect spending on health and schools, risk giving a misleading impression of what public service spending under a Conservative government would look like (Crawford et al, 2015, p 38).

[4] The theory was that the boost to business confidence given by cutting welfare benefits would more than offset their contractionary effects on demand. This is sometimes known as the 'Alesina effect' after its main advocate, Alberto Alesina of Bocconi University in Milan (Skidelsky, 2015). 'Austerians' argue that fiscal stimulus absorbs resources that would otherwise have been used by private firms. Moreover, firms and households would, in all probability, save their share of the proceeds, rather than bolster the economy by spending them, since they would assume that the government's largesse was only temporary and that tax bills would soon go back up (Beddoes, 2014, p 51).

[5] The Eurozone, like the UK, has been pursuing a 'hybrid' policy combining fiscal austerity (also known as fiscal consolidation) with monetary expansion (low interest rates and QE). Austerians resist fiscal stimulus but support QE. QE drives up the price of assets, especially financial assets, and so benefits wealthy households more than it does poor households, who bear the brunt of austerity. In the absence of what social scientists call a 'counter-factual', it is not really possible to say what the effects of a policy of fiscal austerity *tout court* would have been.

[6] The initial expectation was that sharing the euro would promote economic growth and prosperity by making member states' economies converge in terms of productivity and output through inescapable pressure generated by

the single currency to adjust public spending and labour costs internally. An automatic adjustment of imbalances across regions and countries would take place either through the lowering of wages and prices in the less prosperous countries, or through outward migration of labour to more prosperous ones. This is how, according to orthodox economic theory, austerity is supposed to work in a Eurozone member state such as Ireland with an 'open' economy:

> ... a permanent reduction in government spending or higher taxes will increase unemployment, which will reduce wages and prices. This will improve competitiveness, leading to higher external demand for Ireland's products (and less imports) that will eventually replace the lost demand due to austerity. However, because wages and prices are "sticky", this adjustment will not happen quickly. (Wren-Lewis, 2015b)

In the event, the single currency has divided the Eurozone into 'winners' (Germany and other 'surplus' countries in the Northern 'core') and 'losers' (the 'deficit' countries in the Southern and Western peripheries, who no longer have the option of restoring competitiveness through currency devaluation (Offe, 2015, pp 19-27).

[7] The sequester is a series of year-on-year cuts to federal government spending mandated by earlier legislation that came into effect in 2013.

[8] The Maastricht Treaty established the Stability and Growth Pact, which was designed to impose financial discipline on member states by allowing a maximum *fiscal deficit*-to-GDP ratio of 3 per cent and a (*public*) *debt* to GDP ratio of 60 per cent.

[9] The EU2, which is de facto running Europe at the time of writing (September 2015), consists of the German Chancellor, Angela Merkel, the French President, François Hollande, as well as the President of the European Commission, Jean-Claude Juncker, and the heads of the ECB, Mario Draghi, and IMF, Christine Lagarde – these three constituting the Troika – together with the Euro Group (the national finance ministers of the Eurozone countries, personified by Germany's Wolfgang Schäuble).

[10] The Versailles Treaty (1919) brought an end to the First World War. The terms of the peace treaty imposed an unrealistically huge burden of reparation (austerity) on Germany, which had no role in the negotiations. John Maynard Keynes was a British delegate at the Versailles Conference.

[11] This is a reference to the election in Greece in January 2015 of a government led by the anti-austerity Syriza (coalition of the radical left). The ECB's action followed hard on the rejection by the Greek people, in a referendum held on 5 July 2015, of the terms of the bailout.

[12] In German, the word *schuld* means both 'debt' and 'guilt'.

[13] According to the Bank for International Settlements, by 2010 when the crisis hit, French banks held the equivalent of nearly €465 billion in so-called impaired periphery assets, while German banks had €493 billion on their books (figures cited in Blyth, 2015).

[14] The Austrian chapter of the anti-globalisation movement Attac has claimed that over three-quarters went to the financial sector, of which 28 per cent was used to recapitalise Greek banks, 50 per cent went to creditors of the Greek state, and the remainder was an incentive (sweetener) to secure creditors' agreement to take a 'haircut' in March 2012. Just over one-fifth of the first two loans (22 per cent) went to the Greek national budget (to be used, that is, to support the Greek people) or could not be definitively attributed (figures cited in Feifer, 2015).

[15] Remarkably, the Greek Constitution contains a tax exemption clause for wealthy ship-owning families, introduced in 1967. It is argued that attempts to end this exemption would simply lead the ship owners to transfer their wealth and business abroad (Streeck, 2014, p 76).

[16] The Greek electorate's rejection of the two established clientelistic parties, PASOK and New Democracy, was confirmed in a snap parliamentary election in September 2015. Syriza fell short of an absolute majority but was able to renew its coalition with the Independent Greeks (Anel), a right-wing, anti-austerity party. Voter turnout, at just under 57 per cent, was the lowest recorded in a parliamentary election since the restoration of democracy in 1974 (Wikipedia, Greek legislative election, September 2015).

The noted US economist Jeffrey Sachs has commented that a smart creditor of Greece would want to ask how it could help that country to get credit moving again within the banking system, and help promote Greek exports and the growth of small and medium-size enterprises to replace the lost demand due to austerity. These are questions that Greece's creditors, led by Germany, have not asked. Instead, their approach has been to extend new loans so that Greece can service its existing debts (Sachs, 2015).

SIX

Finance-led capitalism at a crossroads?

This is the essence of secular stagnation – sick recoveries which die in their infancy and depressions which feed on themselves and leave a hard and seemingly immovable core of unemployment. (Extract from Alvin Hansen's Presidential address to the American Economic Association, 1938, reproduced in the March 1939 issue of the *American Economic Review*)

This final chapter focuses on three interrelated themes. The first section considers, with particular reference to the UK, the nature of the recovery now under way in many Western countries in the wake of the Great Recession. The second takes stock of what, if anything, has been done about the 'too big to fail' banks. And the third section asks whether the crisis is really over.

A slow recovery

Several years on from the crash, and it is clear that there has been a return to growth in much of the Western world, including the US, UK, and even the Eurozone.[1] The recovery has been slow in coming, and there may well be an underlying reason for this, as set out below.

But the nature and timing of recovery also depends on country-specific factors, and this is a task for specialists to comment on and evaluate. I confine myself here to presenting some data relating to the nature of the recovery occurring in the country with which I am most familiar, the UK.

At the time of writing (September 2015), what I think can best be described as a fragile recovery has been in place in the UK for some two-and-a-half years, with economic output at last surpassing its pre-crisis peak, and unemployment falling to 1.91 million, or 5.8 per cent of the adult population, in the three months to the end of November 2014, according to the ONS. When the great financial crash hit, the unemployment rate was a little over 5 per cent, or 1.6 million. Towards the end of 2009, it was almost a million higher, at 2.5 million, or 8 per cent. Unemployment peaked at almost 2.7 million at the end of 2011.

The pain of the recession has also been spread widely through lower wages,[2] although real wages, too, were 1 per cent higher in the final quarter of 2014 than a year earlier. Before then, they had been falling for seven consecutive years, and remained nearly 7 per cent below their 2007 level (*The Economist*, 2014). Falling real wages is a principal reason why working-age households are worse off than before the crisis, whereas pensioner households have fared better (Machin, 2015).

Despite the resumption of growth, there is no evidence that the UK economy has been significantly rebalanced in the way anticipated in the coalition government's 2011 'plan for growth', which argued the case for a national economy based on investments and exports. Researchers at the University of Sheffield's Political Economy Research Institute found that the finance and insurance sector was a smaller component of overall output (7.4 per cent in the final quarter of 2014) than before the financial crisis (9.9 per cent in the third quarter of 2007), but that so, too, was the manufacturing sector (9.7 per cent compared to 10.9 per cent). Output in London had grown to 22.1 per cent of overall economic output in 2013, from 21 per cent before the crisis. In the South East it had grown rather more slowly to 14.9 per cent, from 14.3 per cent. Output in all three Northern regions had fallen slightly: from 9.6 per cent of overall economic output before the crisis to 9.3

per cent in 2013 in the North West, from 3.1 per cent to 3.0 per cent in the North East and from 7.1 per cent to 6.7 per cent in Yorkshire and Humberside (SPERI, 2015).

Despite well-documented evidence of recovery in Western economies, there are signs of a growing unease in policy circles that the global economy may not return to the pace of expansion seen before the crash. Indeed, the IMF warns that the Western world could be stuck on a new 'mediocre' growth path with high levels of debt and unemployment. As Elliott (2014) describes it, the IMF message for the rich Western economies is that 'you'll never have it so good again'. Likewise, Lawrence Summers, chief economic adviser to President Obama from 2009 to 2010, has cautioned that the US and other wealthy capitalist democracies may be suffering from 'secular stagnation', fated to oscillate between inadequate growth due to an inability to create sufficient demand in the overall economy, and the emergence of financial bubbles brought about by prolonged low interest rates (Summers, 2013). Andrew Haldane, a senior official at the Bank of England, has echoed these concerns (BBC News, 2014).[3]

The most plausible explanation for this pattern of recovery from the Great Recession is that a period of *balance sheet repair* and constrained consumption has been taking place, which is now coming to an end. Households and firms that have been paying down debt (or saving more) over a number of years are now starting to borrow again (Wren-Lewis, 2015d).

Japan, a super-ageing society with the highest proportion of older adults in the world, is the country of reference here: it experienced a major recession in the early 1990s that turned into a decade-long period of stagnation and debt deflation, where falling prices pushed up the real burden of debts. Likewise, since 2009, it has experienced, along with the Eurozone economies, a series of short, shallow recoveries, followed by repeated drifts into recession.

The economist Richard Koo, based at the Nomura Research Institute in Tokyo, has provided a penetrating analysis of the lessons to be learned by other capitalist democracies from Japan's problems exiting from its 1990 recession (Koo, 2011). Koo's argument is that this was no ordinary recession attributable to fluctuations in the business cycle, but a 'balance sheet' recession driven by deleveraging or the paying down of very high levels of private sector debt – in Japan's case, following the bursting of its debt-financed housing and real estate bubble and the resulting plunge in property prices.

Japan's corporate sector responded by shifting from its traditional role as a large borrower of funds to being a massive repayer of debt. Japanese companies, in other words, began to generate financial surpluses on their balance sheets as income that would otherwise have been spent was devoted to repayment. This act of deleveraging reduced aggregate demand and threw the economy into a very special type of recession. But Japan was able to avoid a depression because government borrowing and spending took the place of private sector borrowing and (investment) spending. Such fiscal action maintained incomes in the private sector and allowed businesses and households to pay down debt. By 2005 the private sector had completed its balance sheet repairs. Although government debt increased by over 90 per cent of GDP during the period from 1990 to 2005, because the private sector was deleveraging, the government's fiscal actions did not lead to 'crowding out' of private sector investment, inflation or skyrocketing interest rates (Koo, 2011, p 23).

Even so, the long time required for the Japanese economy to pull out of its balance sheet recession has brought about a debt 'trauma' of sorts in which the private sector refuses to borrow money even after its balance sheet is fully repaired. This trauma may take years if not decades to overcome, during which time the economy will be operating at less than full potential, and may require continued fiscal support from the government to stay afloat. 'In Japan, where the private sector has grown extremely averse to borrowing after its bitter experience of paying down debt from 1990 to 2005, businesses are not borrowing money in spite of willing lenders and the lowest interest rates in human history' (Koo, 2011, p 34). Japan's experience matters because, suggests Koo, the private sectors in the US, UK and continental Europe (apart from Germany, which did not experience an asset price bubble in the first place) are also undergoing massive deleveraging in spite of record low interest rates. This means that these countries are all in serious balance sheet recessions of the kind first experienced by Japan 20 years ago (Koo, 2011, p 25).

Sovereign debt to annual GDP ratios for June 2014 that are in excess of 100 per cent in the UK (102 per cent), the US (106 per cent) and France (115 per cent), well above those figures in all but one of the PIIGS (Spain, 108 per cent) and 230 per cent in Japan (OECD, 2014), illustrate the continuing 'overhang' of *public* debt, which remains an obstacle to faster recovery (Reinhart and Rogoff, 2013).

Writing in 2012, Philip Coggan suggested that reducing the burden of public or government debt would be a long, slow process characterised by one or more of the following scenarios: inflating the debt away through **financial repression**; stagnation (letting the crisis blow itself out through a long period of little or no growth marked by high unemployment and continuing austerity); and default (outright failure by debtor countries to pay down sovereign debt, leading to debt write-downs, most plausibly in some of the Eurozone countries). According to Coggan, household and corporate debt has been kept in check by the very low level of interest rates, and the only way rates could stay at such levels for an extended period would be in the stagnation scenario. But stagnation, in turn, is only an interim alternative as electorates are likely to reject permanent austerity, making default that much more likely. Inflation eventually results in a currency crisis or in a deep recession if the central bank attempts to bring it back under control, so any of the three outcomes can be expected to result in a further crisis at some stage (Coggan, 2012, pp 255, 288).

A few years on and, in my view, Coggan's analysis stands up pretty well, with one important qualification: thus far, with some notable exceptions, the voting publics of Europe and North America have rewarded political parties pledged to cut public deficits and welfare spending by returning them to office.[4] But support for austerity may, in turn, reflect the way in which national politicians have learned how to frame the terms of electoral debate to their own advantage by successfully selling to the public the 'conventional wisdom' that countries, like households, cannot afford to live beyond their means if they are to remain 'competitive' in a globalised economy.

There has, of course, been widespread popular resistance to austerity, particularly in Southern Europe, with, to cite one notable example, hundreds of thousands of young people taking to the streets in Madrid and other Spanish cities in 2011. The most distinctive feature of such youthful protest is a disdain for mainstream political parties, which are accused of failing to do enough to combat unemployment and austerity (Hooghe, 2012).

In Spain, as in Greece, grassroots protest has led to the formation of a new left-wing political party, Podemos ('We can'). More commonly, popular disaffection has found expression on the political right. Most countries in continental Europe now contain influential parties of the radical right (nationalist, anti-immigration, anti-EU, and sometimes anti-austerity as well) with the potential to dictate the terms of political debate to moderate parties. Europe's proportional representation electoral systems, traditionally geared to producing centrist coalitions, are fragmenting, leaving a void that populist parties have filled (Gray, 2009; Traynor, 2014).

In the UK, the 'first-past-the-post' electoral system worked to the advantage of the SNP, which won 50 per cent of the Scottish vote but 95 per cent of Scottish seats in the 2015 general election, and to the disadvantage of UKIP (the United Kingdom Independence Party), which secured only one parliamentary seat despite nearly four million voters endorsing its call for withdrawal from the EU. The near-wipeout of the Labour Party in its former Scottish stronghold contributed to the election of Jeremy Corbyn as its new leader. Labour under Corbyn is the first big, mainstream European political party to adopt a populist, anti-austerity programme in the manner of Syriza and Podemos.

Tom Clark and Anthony Heath's account of the social impact of the Great Recession, which draws on UK and US data, points to the difficulties in the way of building an anti-austerity electoral coalition in either of these two countries. Likening the impact of the Great Recession to that of a tornado that cuts a selective path across communities and neighbourhoods, their stark assessment is that in hard times the constituency of the 'squeezed but basically safe (middle)' is large, and one that has come to calculate that it is better to throw in its lot with the 'haves' than risk being saddled with tax rises to provide assistance to those who are enduring serious hard times (Clark and Heath, 2015, pp 202-13).

The banks: business as usual?

National governments and parliaments are not immune to populist pressures to make the banks pay for losses incurred by the taxpayer in bailing them out, and, as of June 2014, 16 countries in Europe had introduced a bank levy of one sort or another. These countries include the UK, where in 2011 the coalition government introduced an annual tax on the value of bank balance sheets (as opposed to a tax on pay pots or bonus pools[5]), with the proceeds being used to create an insurance fund to bail out the banks in any future financial crisis. The rationale was to discourage banks from relying on risky forms of borrowing: retail deposits and the first £20 billion of bank debt are exempt, so only the bigger banks, including foreign banks operating in the UK, pay the levy, which was forecast to raise £2.7 billion in 2014-15 (IFS, 2014).[6]

These national variations have given rise to multiple bank levy charges for global banks, adding to pressures for harmonisation. But bank levies are also in tension with the main thrust of banking reform,[7] which is the 're-regulation' agenda of strengthening capital, liquidity and leverage requirements quietly being progressed by the Bank for International Settlements, the Basel Committee on Banking Supervision, the IMF, the Financial Stability Board (FSB) and the G20 as the preferred, technocratic solution to the problem of the big, global banks. These regulatory measures, which include a parallel initiative that would oblige transnational corporations operating in OECD[8] and G20 countries to disclose revenues, profits and taxes on a country by country basis to tax authorities, amount to a repairing and relaunching of the existing banking and financial system under more internationally coordinated conditions.

The bigger issue of whether to break up the 'too big to fail' banks has been ducked, both in the US and in Europe. Johnson and Kwak suggest that the core problem – banks that are both too big to fail and powerful enough to tilt the political landscape in their favour – can only be tackled by passing new legislation imposing a cap on size: no financial institution should be allowed to control or have an ownership interest in assets worth more than a fixed percentage of GDP.[9] Meanwhile, a vague expectation on the part of the big banks that the taxpayer would bail them out in the event of a crisis has been transformed into a virtual certainty, and the incentive structures created by high leverage and big bonuses are, as yet, largely unchanged. It follows that if the basic conditions that created the financial crisis and ensuing global recession remain the same, then the outcome – another crisis of greater or lesser severity than the present one – will also be the same (Johnson and Kwak, 2010, pp 12-13). In short, incremental, technocratic reform is not going to do the job: breaking up the big banks requires decisive action by democratically elected governments, and there is little prospect of this occurring in the foreseeable future.[10]

Is the crisis over?

Deep though the financial and economic crisis has been, it has not so far produced a major shift in the neoliberal policy framework, and it is far from clear whether the crisis and the austerity and deficit reduction policies that have followed in its wake will lead to shifts in assumptions about the role of government and to a major restructuring of the financial system in the manner of previous crises of capitalism in the 1930s and 1970s. Nor would a change in the intellectual climate, for example, the emergence of a compelling counter-narrative to austerity, by itself be enough to displace an established order. Changing the ideas that govern economic policy-making necessarily involves politics and, in the present context, the building of a new coalition of interests capable of challenging the dominance over public life of financial and other transnational corporations (Gamble, 2012).

In hindsight, it is clear that the neo- or post-Fordist accounts developed by the first generation of regulation theorists, based on changes in industrial production and mass consumption, failed to anticipate the changing balance of class forces implicit in finance-led capitalism. The collapse of the Soviet Union and the transformation of China, together with rapid technological change, offshoring and increased immigration in the already developed countries, means that, globally, capital has plenty of cheap labour available to it. Nor, in an era of global financial markets and structural imbalances between Asian producers and Western consumers is organised labour so central to the resolution of the crisis of the current growth model (Mason, 2009, pp 157-73).

Andrew Gamble (2014), writing in the context of the first signs of a recovery in the UK economy, argues that the financial and economic crisis can be interpreted in three ways. The first possibility, that it was just a 'blip' with no long-term significance, echoes the argument of the US National Commission that 'there are some on Wall Street and in Washington with a stake in the status quo who may be tempted to see the events of 2007-08 merely as "bumps in the road" or an accentuated dip in the financial and business cycles that we have come to expect in a free market economy' (Financial Crisis Inquiry Commission, 2011, p xv).

The second possibility is that some kind of watershed has indeed been reached, and that we are now in the early stages of a gradual political and economic transformation which will reorder the international economy and international politics in the course of the next two decades – that the neoliberal order is breaking up and that we are, to sustain the highway metaphor, approaching a new 'crossroads'.

The third possibility is that there has indeed been a fundamental change, but because the immediate crisis has been more or less adequately contained, many of the economic, political and ideological challenges posed by the global financial crisis have been postponed. On this reading, the neoliberal order is remarkably resilient but inherently unstable, and the underlying strains and contradictions will rumble on, with occasional shocks and upheavals, but with no decisive turning point (Gamble, 2014, pp 5-6).

We should bear in mind Paul Mason's admonition that the dominance of finance, derivatives and a debt-fuelled growth model is in reality a fairly recent phenomenon, and that the dynamics of future capitalist growth will be shaped not just by the financial crash and the Great Recession but by the long-term ageing of populations, by climate change, by the rise of Asia, and by the coming decline of the carbon economy (Mason, 2009, p 172). But that said, there are, in my judgement, good grounds for believing, with Gamble, that the most likely possibility for the foreseeable future is that those of us residing in the rich West will continue to live in a neoliberal world dominated by modestly re-regulated financial markets, by consumer debt and by global networks of integrated production orchestrated by transnational corporations, with their transfer pricing and **regulatory arbitrage**. This is because, in Colin Crouch's words:

> … low and medium-wage, insecure workers will not be able to continue spending unless they can get their hands on unsecured credit, even if at less frenetic levels than had been occurring. Governments will want to see a return to credit boom as the most effective way of restoring consumer confidence while they continue to pursue policies making labour markets more flexible. They will be vulnerable to arguments from the financial sector that some relaxation of regulation will be needed if this is to happen. And, in a beggar-my-neighbour competition, individual governments will be tempted to ensure that they have slightly less onerous regulation than the others, in order to attract financial firms to base themselves within their jurisdictions in a competition that clearly leaves the firms in the more powerful position. (Crouch, 2011, pp 120-1)

It begins to look, then, not so much as if we are heading towards a crossroads as that we are at an impasse, destined to remain for the foreseeable future on a path from which there is no real prospect of escape.

Notes

[1] In 2015, GDP growth was expected to exceed 3 per cent in Spain, 5 per cent in Ireland and 1.6 per cent in Portugal (Stewart, 2015, citing IMF figures).

[2] Of the 12 initial signatories of the Maastricht Treaty on European Union (1992), only Greece and Portugal now have lower hourly wages than the UK. The ready supply of cheap labour in continental Europe further encourages hiring – half a million more EU migrants are now employed in the UK than in 2010, accounting for roughly a third of the country's recent employment boom; 70 per cent of those migrants end up in low-skilled jobs. The Bank of England forecasts 3 per cent growth in 2015, but that has a lot to do with low oil prices dragging down inflation, and increased competition for workers. The Bank's forecast for productivity growth (output per hour worked) is a much more modest 0.75 per cent (*The Economist*, 2015).

[3] We should, of course, be wary of forecasts of the future based on trends in the recent past. Secular stagnation – implying that weak growth is a permanent or 'structural' rather than a cyclical phenomenon – is not new, and has been proved wrong before. Alvin Hansen coined the term in his 1938 address: the date is significant because despite a recovery from the Great Depression in the early 1930s, there was a relapse in 1937 (Elliott, 2014). There was much talk, too, of secular stagnation at the end of the Second World War, yet during the next three decades, the global economy expanded at rates not seen previously.

[4] In Scotland the left-leaning, anti-austerity Scottish Nationalist Party (SNP) won 56 out of 59 seats north of the border in the May 2015 UK general election. As suggested in Chapter Five, voters in Germany, and in much of the rest of Europe, see the Eurozone debt crisis in redistributive terms, according to which they are subsidising other countries less virtuous than themselves. US elections in November 2014 saw sweeping gains by the Republican Party in the Senate, the House of Representatives and numerous state governorship elections.

In Canada, the centre-left Liberal Party won a decisive victory in the October 2015 federal election, ending nearly a decade of Conservative rule. The Liberals campaigned on a pledge to run three consecutive (modest) budget deficits, and to introduce a new, higher tax rate on income over $200,000, to help fund infrastructure spending and tax cuts for middle-income Canadians. The Party also said it would balance the federal budget by 2019. On the face of it, the result was an emphatic rejection of the fiscal austerity that was the hallmark of the previous Conservative administrations, but the different fiscal context of Canada, compared to countries more severely hit by the Great Recession, needs to be borne in mind: the 2014-15 federal budget showed a small surplus, not a sizeable deficit as in the US or UK. Unsurprisingly, a pledge to relax austerity proved attractive to voters.

[5] In April 2013 the European Parliament approved the text of Capital Requirements Directive IV, which, among other things, imposes a cap on the level of bankers' bonuses. In a notable and quite possibly Pyrrhic victory for the directly elected assembly in its tug of war with the European Commission, reform of bankers' remuneration was demanded in return for Parliament agreeing to the rest of the legislation, which is designed to bring Europe's financial institutions in line with the Basel 111 rules. Bankers' bonuses are capped at one year's salary, although member states can double that with the approval of bank shareholders. The concession to the UK government and the City, which opposed the measure on the grounds that the bonus cap would be self-defeating because bankers' fixed pay would now rise even faster, was to also agree to the use of longer-term share options as perks for bank employees (Bowers et al, 2013).

[6] The new Conservative government announced, in its July 2015 Budget, that the bank levy would be gradually cut from 0.21 per cent to 0.1 per cent in 2021, by which time it would apply to banks' UK balance sheets only. In its place, a new, 8 per cent surcharge on bank profits will be introduced from 1 January 2016. Treasury estimates suggest the new profit surcharge and the changes to the levy will bring in about £1.7 billion in extra revenue over the next five years.

[7] This is because levies limit each bank's ability to build up capital reserves from retained earnings.

[8] The OECD (Organisation for Economic Co-operation and Development) is a forum where the governments of 34 capitalist democracies in North and South America, Europe and the Asia-Pacific region work with each other to promote economic growth and sustainable development.

[9] Johnson and Kwak's 'first proposal' specifies a cap on the size of US commercial banks of no more than 4 per cent of US GDP, and for Wall Street investment banks such as Goldman Sachs, a size limit of 2 per cent of GDP. The proposal anticipates that the limits should be set by Congress and then enforced by regulators. Banks could choose to operate globally or only in the US, but in either case, the size limit would be set relative to the performance of the US economy, and offshore activities would count toward the limit (Johnson and Kwak, 2010, pp 214-5). Simon Johnson, it should be noted, is a former chief economist at the IMF.

[10] In the fourth quarter of 2014, the five largest banks held 46 per cent of US banking assets and 40 per cent of domestic deposits, up from 28 per cent and 20 per cent, respectively, in the first quarter of 2000. The number of small US banks (with US$10 billion or less in assets) has declined from 8,263 in the first quarter of 2000 to 5,961 in the fourth quarter in 2014 (Peirce and Miller, 2015).

References

Admati, A. and Hellwig, M. (2013) *The bankers' new clothes*, Princeton, NJ: Princeton University Press.

Aglietta, M. (1982) 'World capitalism in the eighties', *New Left Review*, vol 136, pp 5-41 (at p 25).

Ahamed, L. (2014) 'How banks fail, *The New York Times*, 13 April.

Allaire, Y. and Firsirotu, M. (2014) *Inequality and executive compensation: A US problem but what about Quebec and Canada?*, Montreal, Canada: Institute for Governance of Private and Public Organizations (IGOPP) (www.igopp.org).

Alvaredo, F., Atkinson, A., Piketty, T. and Saez, E. (nd) *The world top incomes database* (http://topincomes.g-mond.parisschoolofeconomics.eu).

Amin, A., Cameron, A. and Hudson, R. (2002) *Placing the social economy*, London: Routledge.

Appelbaum, E. and Batt, R. (2010) 'Financialization and the jobless recovery', *Insight* (www.insightweb.it).

Armstrong, P., Glyn, A. and Harrison, J. (1991) *Capitalism since 1945*, Oxford: Blackwell.

Atkinson, A. (2013) 'UK estimates of top income shares 2010-2011; note on methods', in F. Alvaredo, A. Atkinson, T. Piketty and E. Saez, *The world top incomes database* (http://topincomes.g-mond.parisschoolofeconomics.eu).

Augar, P. (2010) *Reckless*, London: Vintage Books.

Bank of England (nd) 'Quantitative easing explained', London: Bank of England (www.bankofengland.co.uk/monetarypolicy/Documents/pdf/qe-pamphlet.pdf).

BBC News (2013) 'What is quantitative easing?', 7 March.

BBC News (2014) 'Slow economic growth to be "prolonged", says Bank economist', 24 November (*bbc.co.uk/news/business-30186390*).

Beddoes, Z. (2014) *Debts, deficits and dilemmas*, London: Profile Books.

Bell, S. and Hindmoor, A. (2015) *Masters of the universe, slaves of the market*, Cambridge, MA: Harvard University Press.

Bernanke, B. (2007) 'Regulation and financial innovation', Speech delivered at the Federal Reserve Bank of Atlanta's financial markets conference (www.federalreserve.gov).

BIS (Bank for International Settlements) (2009) *Report on special purpose entities,* Basel, Switzerland: BIS (www.bis.org).

Blyth, M. (2013) *Austerity*, New York: Oxford University Press.

Blyth, M. (2015) 'A pain in the Athens', *Foreign Affairs*, 7 July (www.foreignaffairs.com).

Blyth, M. and Lonergan, E. (2014) 'Print less but transfer more', *Foreign Affairs*, vol 93, no 5, pp 98-109.

Bootle, R. (2012) *The trouble with markets*, London: Nicholas Brealey Publishing.

Bowers, S., Treanor, J., Walsh, F., Finch, J., Collinson, P. and Treanor, I. (2013) 'Bonuses: the essential guide', *The Guardian*, 28 February.

Brooks, R. (2013) *The great tax robbery*, London: One World.

Calomiris, C. and Haber. S. (2014) *Fragile by design: The political origins of banking crises and scarce credit*, Princeton, NJ: Princeton University Press.

Chandler, A. (1984) 'The emergence of market capitalism', *Business History Review*, vol 58, pp 473-503.

Chang, H.-J. (2007) *Bad Samaritans*, London: Random House.

Chang, H.-J. (2013) 'Another financial crisis looms if rich countries can't kick their addiction to cash injection', *The Guardian*, 30 August.

Chang, H.-J. (2014) *Economics: The user's guide*, London: Pelican.

Clark, D. (2002) 'Neoliberalism and public service reform: Canada in comparative perspective', *Canadian Journal of Political Science*, vol 35, no 4, pp 771-93.

Clark, D. (2004) 'Implementing the third way: modernising government and public services in Quebec and the UK', *Public Management Review*, vol 6, no 4, pp 493-510.

Clark, T. and Heath, A. (2015) *Hard times: Inequality, recession, aftermath*, London: Yale University Press.

Coggan, P. (2009) *The money machine* (6th edn), London: Penguin.

Coggan, P. (2012) *Paper promises*, London: Penguin.

Conyon, M. and Sadler, G. (2010) 'Shareholder voting and directors' remuneration report legislation: say on pay in the UK', *Corporate Governance: An International Review*, vol 18, no 4, pp 296-312.

Crawford, R., Emmerson, C., Keynes, S. and Tetlow, G. (2015) *Post-election austerity: Parties' plans compared*, London: Nuffield Foundation and Institute for Fiscal Studies.

Crossley, T. and O'Dea, C. (2010) *The wealth and saving of UK families on the eve of the crisis*, London: Institute for Fiscal Studies.

Crouch, C. (1982) *The politics of industrial relations* (2nd edn), London: Fontana.

Crouch, C. (2011) *The strange non-death of neoliberalism*, Cambridge: Polity.

Davidson, A. (2008) 'How AIG fell apart', *Reuters*, 18 September.

Davies, H. (2010) *The financial crisis*, Cambridge: Polity.

Davies, H. (2015) *Can financial markets be controlled?*, Cambridge: Polity.

Dorling, D. (2014) *Inequality and the 1%*, London: Verso.

Dyson, K. (2015) 'The morality of debt', *Foreign Affairs*, 3 May (www.foreignaffairs.com).

Economist, The (2014) 'What recovery?', 25 October (www.economist.com/news/britain/21627665-workers-continue-feel-pinch-what-recovery).

Economist, The (2015) 'Bargain basement', 14 March (www.economist.com/news/britain/21646235-if-britain-cannot-get-more-its-legion-cheap-workers-recovery-will-stall-bargain).

Elliott, L. (2014) 'IMF goes back to the future with gloomy talk of secular stagnation', *The Guardian*, 7 October.

Engelen, E., Erturk, I., Johal, S., Leaver, A., Moran, M., Nilsson, A. and Williams, K. (2011) *After the great complacence*, Oxford: Oxford University Press.

Fazi, T. (2014) *The battle for Europe*, London: Pluto Press.

Feifer, G. (2015) 'Merkel's misstep', *Foreign Affairs*, 28 July (www. foreignaffairs.com).

Ferguson, C. (2014) *Inside job*, London: One World.

Financial Crisis Inquiry Commission (2011) *The financial crisis inquiry report, including dissenting views*, New York: Cosimo.

Fleming, P. (2008) 'Managerial capitalism', in S. Clegg and J. Bailey (eds) *International encyclopedia of organization studies*, London: Sage, pp 864-5.

Froud, J., Nilsson, A., Moran, M. and Williams, K. (2012) 'Stories and interests in finance: agendas of governance before and after the financial crisis', *Governance*, vol 25, no 1, pp 35-59.

FSB (Financial Stability Board) (2014) '2014 update of list of global systemically important banks (G-SIBs)', 6 November (www. financialstabilityboard.org/wp-content/uploads/r_141106b.pdf).

Galbraith, J.K. (1967) *The new industrial state*, London: Hamish Hamilton.

Galbraith, J.K. (2009). 'Who are these economists, anyway?', *Thought and Action*, vol 25, pp 85-95.

Gamble, A. (1994) *The free economy and the strong state*, Basingstoke: Macmillan.

Gamble, A. (2009) *The spectre at the feast*, Basingstoke: Palgrave Macmillan.

Gamble, A. (2011) *Economic futures*, London: British Academy.

Gamble, A. (2012) 'Have the social sciences failed us?', London: British Academy (www.britac.ac.uk).

Gamble, A. (2014) *Crisis without end?*, Basingstoke: Palgrave Macmillan.

Garton Ash, T. (2008) 'The US democratic-capitalist model is on trial. No schadenfreude, please', *The Guardian*, 1 September.

Giddens, A. (2014) *Turbulent and mighty continent*, Cambridge: Polity.

Grant, W. and Wilson, G. (eds) (2014) *The consequences of the global financial crisis: The rhetoric of reform and regulation*, Oxford: Oxford University Press.

Gray, J. (2009) *False dawn,* London: Granta.

Guttmann, R. (2008) 'A primer on finance-led capitalism and its crisis', *Revue de la régulation,* nos 3 and 4, December (https://regulation.revues.org/5843).

Hacker, J. and Pierson, P. (2011) *Winner-take-all politics*, New York: Simon & Schuster.

Hall, P. and Soskice, D. (2001) *Varieties of capitalism*, Oxford: Oxford University Press.

Hansen, A. (1939) 'Economic progress and declining population growth', *American Economic Review*, vol 29, no 1, pp 1-15.

Harris, L. (1988) 'The UK economy at a crossroads', in J. Allen and D. Massey (eds) *The economy in question*, London: Sage, 7-44.

Haltom, R. (2014) 'Why was Canada exempt from the financial crisis?', *Econ Focus, Federal Reserve Bank of Richmond*, Fourth Quarter, pp 22-5.

Harvey, D. (2007) *A brief history of neoliberalism*, New York: Oxford University Press.

Harvey, D. (2014) *Seventeen contradictions and the end of capitalism*, London: Profile Books.

Hills, J. (2015) *Good times, bad times*, Bristol: Policy Press.

Hooghe, M. (2012) 'Taking to the streets: economic crisis and youth protest in Europe' *Harvard International Review*, vol 34, no 2 (hir.harvard.edu).

Hopkin, J. (2015) 'The troubled south: the euro experience in Italy and Spain', in M. Matthijs and M. Blyth (eds) *The future of the euro*, New York: Oxford University Press, pp 161-84.

Hutton, W. (2014) 'Banking is changing, slowly, but its culture is still corrupt', *The Observer*, 16 November.

Hutton, W. (2015) *How good we can be: Ending the mercenary society and building a great country*, London: Little, Brown & Co.

IFS (Institute for Fiscal Studies) (2014) *A survey of the UK tax system*, London: IFS.

IMF (International Monetary Fund) (2010) *Understanding financial interconnectedness*, Washington, DC: IMF (www.imf.org).

IMF (2015) *Greece: An update of IMF Staff's preliminary public debt sustainability analysis*, IMF Country Report No 15/186, Washington, DC: IMF (www.imf.org).

Jessop, R. (2002) *The future of the capitalist state*, Cambridge: Polity.

Jessop, R. and Sum, N.-L. (2006) *Beyond the regulation approach*, Cheltenham: Edward Elgar Publishing.

Johnson, S. and Kwak, J. (2010) *13 bankers*, New York: Pantheon.

Julius, D. (2008) *Public Services Industry Review*, London: Department for Business, Enterprise and Regulatory Reform, www.berr.gov.uk.

Kaletsky, A. (2010) *Capitalism 4.0*, London: Bloomsbury.

Kay, J. (2004) *The truth about markets*, London: Penguin.

Kay, J. (2012) *Review of UK equity markets and long-term decision making*, London: Department for Business, Innovation and Skills, July.

Keen, S. (2012) *The debtwatch manifesto* (www.debtdeflation.com/blogs/manifesto).

Keynes, J.M. (1920) *The economic consequences of the peace*, New York: Harcourt, Brace & Howe.

Koo, R. (2011) 'The world in balance sheet recession: causes, cure and politics', *Real-World Economics Review*, vol 58, pp 19-37.

Krippner, G. (2012) *Capitalizing on crisis*, Cambridge, MA: Harvard University Press.

Krugman, P. (2009) 'How did economists get it so wrong?', *The New York Times*, 2 September.

Krugman, P. (2012) *End this depression now!*, New York: W.W. Norton & Co.

Kundnani, H. (2015) 'The return of the German question: why conflict between creditor and debtor states is now the defining feature of European politics', LSE Blog, 26 January, London: London School of Economics and Political Science (http://blogs.lse.ac.uk/europpblog/).

Kynaston, D. (2012) *City of London: The history*, London: Vintage Books.

Lanchester, J. (2008) 'Cityphilia', *London Review of Books*, vol 30, no 1, pp 9-12.

Lash, S. and Urry, J. (1987) *The end of organised capitalism,* Cambridge: Polity.

Laskaridis, C (2014) *False dilemmas: A critical guide to the eurozone crisis,* Corporate Watch (www.corporatewatch.org).

Lazonick, W. (2009), *Sustainable prosperity in the new economy?,* Kalamazoo, MI: W.E. Upjohn Institute for Employment Research.

Lazonick, W. (2010) 'Innovative business models and varieties of capitalism: financialization of the US corporation', *Business History Review,* vol 84, no 4, pp 675-702.

Lazonick, W. (2013) 'The financialization of the US corporation: what has been lost, and how it can be regained', *Seattle University Law Review,* vol 36, pp 857-909.

Lazonick, W. and Mazzucato, M. (2012) *The risk-reward nexus,* London: Policy Network.

Legrain, P. (2015) 'The Eurozone has become a glorified debtors' prison', *Social Europe,* 17 March.

Lewis, M. (2014) *Flash boys,* New York: W.W. Norton & Co.

Livesey, B. (2013) *Thieves of Bay Street,* Toronto, Canada: Random House.

Lowe, S. (2011) *The housing debate,* Bristol: Policy Press.

Luttrell, D., Rosenblum, H., and Jackson, T. (2012) *Understanding the risks inherent in shadow banking: A primer and practical lessons learned,* Staff Papers, Dallas, TX: Federal Reserve Bank of Dallas (www.dallasfed.org/assets/documents/research/staff/staff1203.pdf).

McLeay, M., Radia, A. and Thomas, R. (2014) 'Money creation in the modern economy', *Bank of England Q1 Quarterly Bulletin* (www.bankofengland.co.uk).

McNamara, K. (2015) 'Europe after the Greek debt crisis', *Foreign Affairs,* 19 July (www.foreignaffairs.com).

Machin, S. (2015) *Real wages and living standards: Latest UK evidence,* London: Centre for Economic Performance, London School of Economics and Political Science (cep.lse.ac.uk).

Malgesine, G. (2014) 'Spain', in The European Anti-Poverty Network, *Lifeboat or life sentence?,* Brussels: The European Anti-Poverty Network (www.eapn.eu).

Martin, A., Kersley, H. and Greenham, T. (2014) *Inequality and financialisation: A dangerous mix,* London and Berlin: New Economics Foundation/Friedrich-Ebert-Stiftung.

Mason, P. (2009) *Meltdown,* London: Verso.

Massey, D. (2013) 'The ills of financial dominance', *Open Democracy,* 24 September.

Mazzucato, M. (2014) 'Smart countries are the ones creating and shaping their own markets', *The Observer,* 21 July.

Meisel, J. (1958) *The myth of the ruling class,* Ann Arbor, MI: University of Michigan Press.

Moran, M. (2009) *Business, politics and society,* Oxford: Oxford University Press.

Moran, M. (2013) 'The banking crisis as an elite debacle – again', LSE Blog, London: London School of Economics and Political Science (http://blogs.lse.ac.uk/politicsandpolicy/the-banking-crisis-as-an-elite-debacle-again/).

Moravcsik, A. (2012) 'Europe after the crisis', *Foreign Affairs,* vol 91, no 3, pp 54-68.

OECD (Organisation for Economic Co-operation and Development) (2014) *Government debt: Key tables from OECD, no 21,* Paris: OECD (www.oecd-library.org).

Nakamoto, M. and Wighton, D. (2007) 'Citigroup chief stays bullish on buy-outs', *The Financial Times,* 9 July.

Offe, C. (2015) *Europe entrapped,* Cambridge: Polity.

Oltermann, P. (2015) 'Jürgen Habermas's verdict on the EU/Greece debt deal', *The Guardian,* 16 July.

O'Rourke, K. (2015) 'Moving on from the euro', *Social Europe,* 23 July.

Palier, B. (ed) (2010) *A long goodbye to Bismarck?,* Amsterdam: Amsterdam University Press.

Panitch, L. and Gindin, S. (2013) *The making of global capitalism,* London: Verso.

Pappos, T. (2010) 'The causes of the Greek crisis are in Greek politics', *Open Democracy,* 29 November.

Parramore, L. (2014) 'William Lazonick: how superstar companies like Apple are killing America's high-tech future', Institute for New Economic Thinking *(ineteconomics.org)*.

Peck, J. (2012) *Constructions of neoliberal reason*, Oxford: Oxford University Press.

Peirce, H. and Miller, M. (2015) *Small banks by the numbers, 2000-2014*, Arlington, VA: Mercatus Center, George Mason University.

Peston, R. (2014) 'What happens when the PPI cash runs out?', BBC News, 7 July (www.bbc.co.uk/news/business).

Peston, R. and Knight, L. (2012) *How do we fix this mess?*, London: Hodder.

Peters, B.G. (1999) *Institutional theory in political science*, London: Continuum.

Pierson, P. (1994) *Dismantling the welfare state*, Cambridge: Cambridge University Press.

Pierson, P. (1996) 'The new politics of the welfare state', *World Politics*, vol 48, no 2, pp 143-79.

Posen, A. (2013) 'What next?', *Prospect*, January, pp 36-7.

Positive Money (nd) 'How is money really made by banks' (http://positivemoney.org/how-money-works/banking-101-video-course/how-is-money-really-made-by-banks-banking-101-part-3/).

Prabha, A., Savard, K. and Wickramarachi, H. (2014) 'Derivatives: wmd (weapons of mass destruction) or insurance?', *The Milken Institute Review* (www.milkeninstitute.org).

Quiggin, J. (2010) *Zombie economics: How dead ideas still walk among us*, Princeton, NJ: Princeton University Press.

Rajan, R. (2010) *Fault lines*, Princeton, NJ: Princeton University Press.

Regan, A. (2013) *The 'one size fits all' approach risks intensifying Europe's north-south divide*, London: Policy Network.

Reinhart, C. and Rogoff, K. (2013) *Financial and sovereign debt crises: Some lessons learned and those forgotten*, IMF Working Paper 13/266, Washington, DC: IMF (www.imf.org).

Reinhart, C. and Sbrancia, M.B. (2011) *The liquidation of government debt*, Cambridge, MA: National Bureau of Economic Research.

Roubini, N. and Mihm, S. (2011) *Crisis economics*, London: Penguin.

Rowlingson, K. (2012) *Wealth inequality: Key facts*, Birmingham: University of Birmingham Policy Commission on the Distribution of Wealth.

Runciman, D. (2011) 'Didn't they notice?', *London Review of Books*, vol 33, no 8, pp 20-3.

Ryan-Collins, J., Greenham, T., Werner, R. and Jackson, A. (2014) *Where does money come from? A guide to the UK money and banking system* (2nd edn), London: New Economics Foundation.

Sachs, J. (2015) 'Germany, Greece and the future of Europe', *Social Europe*, 21 July.

Sayer, A. (2015) *Why we can't afford the rich*, Bristol: Policy Press.

Scott, B. (2013) *The heretic's guide to global finance*, London: Pluto Press.

Sen, A. (2015) 'The economic consequences of austerity', *New Statesman*, 4 June.

Shaxson, N. (2012) *Treasure islands*, London: Vintage Books.

Sikka, P. (2014) *Banking in the public interest*, London: Centre for Labour and Social Studies (classonline.org.uk).

Skidelsky, R. (2015) 'George Osborne's cunning plan: how the chancellor's austerity narrative has harmed recovery', *New Statesman*, 29 April.

Smith, S. (2009) 'Wall Street rocket scientists crash to earth' (www. phys.org/news/2009-04-wall-street-rocket-scientists-earth-html).

Smith, Y. (2011) *ECONned: How unenlightened self-interest undermined democracy and corrupted capitalism*, New York: Palgrave Macmillan.

SPERI (Sheffield Political Economy Research Institute) (2015) *Has the UK economy been rebalanced?*, Sheffield: SPERI, University of Sheffield (http://speri.dept.shef.ac.uk/).

Stanford, J. (2008) 'When the buck stops', *Red Pepper*, June/July.

Stewart, H. (2015) 'Dublin, Lisbon and Madrid have beaten the bailout. That's no comfort to Athens', *The Guardian*, 18 July.

Stiglitz, J. (2010) *Freefall: America, free markets, and the sinking of the world economy*, New York: W.W. Norton & Co.

Stiglitz, J. (2015) 'Europe's attack on democracy', *Social Europe*, 29 July.

Stockhammer, E. (2014) 'Foreword', in A. Martin et al, *Inequality and financialisation: A dangerous mix*, London and Berlin: New Economics Foundation/Friedrich-Ebert-Stiftung, p 2.

Streeck, W. (2014) *Buying time*, London: Verso.

Summers, L. (2013) 'Economic stagnation is not our fate – unless we want it to be', *The Washington Post*, 18 December.

Taylor-Gooby, P. (2011) 'Foreword', in A. Gamble, *Economic futures*, London: British Academy (www.britac.ac.uk).

Tett, G. (2009) *Fool's gold*, London: Little, Brown & Co.

Thompson, H. (2009) 'The political origins of the financial crisis: the domestic and international politics of Fannie Mae and Freddie Mac', *The Political Quarterly*, vol 80, no 1, pp 17-24.

Thompson, H. (2013) 'The dirty little secret of the eurozone crisis: the German banks', SPERI blog, Sheffield: Sheffield Political Economy Research Institute, University of Sheffield, 11 November (http://speri.dept.shef.ac.uk/2013/11/11/dirty-secret-euro-zone-crisis-german-banks/).

Traynor, I. (2014) 'The centre is falling apart across Europe', *The Observer*, 16 November.

TUC (Trades Union Congress) (2015) *Outsourcing public services*, London: TUC and the New Economics Foundation.

Turner, A. (2013) 'Debt, money and Mephistopheles: how do we get out of this mess?', Financial Conduct Authority, Speech first delivered at the Cass Business School, London.

Turner, A. (2015) 'The social value of finance: problems and solutions', in M. Mazzucato and C. Penna (eds) *Mission-oriented finance for innovation*, London: Policy Network, pp 21-29.

Turner, G. (2008) *The credit crunch,* London: Pluto Press.

Urry, J. (2014) *Offshoring*, Cambridge: Polity.

US (United States) SEC (Securities and Exchange Commission) (2013) 'Agencies issue final rules implementing the Volcker rule', Press Release 2013-58, Washington, DC: US SEC (www.sec.gov/News/PressRelease/Detail/PressRelease/1370540476526).

Veall, M. (2012) 'Top income shares in Canada: recent trends and policy implications', *Canadian Journal of Economics*, vol 45, no 4, pp 1247-72.

Walks, A. and Clifford, B. (2015) 'The political economy of mortgage securitization and the neoliberalization of housing policy in Canada', *Environment and Planning A*, advance online publication.

Watkins, S. (2013) 'Vanity and venality', *London Review of Books*, vol 35, no 16, pp 17-21.

Werner, R. (2012) 'How to make banks socially useful: the case for local banking and local money', Centre for Banking, Finance & Sustainable Development, University of Southampton (www.justbanking.org.uk/wp-content/uploads/Edinburgh-Werner-Case-for-Local-Banks-2012.pdf).

Wilcox, S. (2014) *Housing benefit size criteria: Impacts for social sector tenants and options for reform*, York: Joseph Rowntree Foundation.

Wilks, S. (2013) *The political power of the business corporation*, Cheltenham: Edward Elgar Publishing.

Wilkinson, R. and Pickett, K. (2009) *The spirit level: Why more equal societies almost always do better*, London: Allen Lane.

Wolf, M. (2014) *The shifts and the shocks*, London: Allen Lane.

Wray, R. (2015) 'Dispelling myths about government deficits', in M. Mazzucato and C. Penna (eds) *Mission-oriented finance for innovation*, London: Policy Network, pp 39-48.

Wren-Lewis, S. (2015a) 'The austerity con', *London Review of Books*, vol 37, no 4, pp 9-11.

Wren-Lewis, S. (2015b) 'Ireland and Greece', 19 July (mainlymacro.blogspot.com).

Wren-Lewis, S. (2015c) 'The Great Recession and the Eurozone', 12 July (mainlymacro.blogspot.com).

Wren-Lewis, S. (2015d) 'Is deficit fetishism innate or contextual?', 4 August (mainlymacroblogspot.com).

APPENDIX
A rough guide to global finance

Algorithmic trading In mathematics and computer science, an algorithm is a process or set of rules to be followed in calculations or other problem-solving operations. Algorithmic trading is the process of using computers programmed to follow a defined set of instructions to place a trade at a speed and frequency that is impossible for a human trader (Investopedia; see also Lewis, 2014, a best-selling exposé of high speed trading).

Assets An asset is anything that can be bought or sold on a financial market. To a bank, its loans are assets because they generate interest. Assets that can be easily converted into cash, such as no-notice bank savings accounts or shares that can be bought or sold on a stock exchange, are known as *liquid* assets. From an investor's point of view, an asset's value is set in anticipation of some future stream of revenue or some future state of scarcity (for example, of gold). The outcome of investment flows into tradeable financial assets in the years preceding the 2008 crash was a general rise in asset values (land, property, commodities and so on), and the creation of new asset markets within the financial system itself (Harvey, 2014, p 240).

Asset-backed commercial paper (ABCP) 'Commercial paper' (CP) is short-term debt, typically lasting not more than a year and often for three months, issued by large corporations with excellent credit ratings. They use the cash raised through the sale of CP to finance day-to-day operations and short-term liabilities. Investors who buy the paper are making short-term loans to these corporations backed only by the promise to pay the face amount on the maturity date specified on the note (paper). Other corporations arrange for banks to sell CP on their behalf via a conduit or special purpose vehicle (SPV). Although a short-term operation, CP is issued as part of a continuous rolling programme (Wikipedia).

The length of the debt makes ABCP similar to CP, but ABCP is different because it is backed by the cash flow generated by pools of assets such as trade receivables (money owed by customers in exchange for goods or services that have been delivered but not yet paid for), student loans or bank loans for business expansion. For example, a bank might decide to sell its credit card balances, a manufacturing firm its trade receivable balances or the financing arm of a car company the future stream of payments on its car loans. A suitably large portfolio is assembled and transferred to the conduit/SPV, which will, in turn, fund the purchase by issuing ABCP which is then bought and sold in the short-term money markets to institutional investors such as pension funds and money market funds (MMFs) looking to maximise their return on short-term cash deposits.

On the maturity date of the ABCP, the originating company or bank buys back the underlying assets at a previously agreed price that is higher than that at which it sold them. This money is used to pay back the investors who hold the paper at maturity, or they may be repaid by the issuance of further ABCP (see http://shadowbanking. weebly.com/asset-backed-commercial-paper.html).

Asset bubble This arises when an asset trades in large volumes at prices higher than its intrinsic value. Rising prices generate increasing interest in investing in that market, which further increases prices to an unsustainable level. Bubbles are often associated with an excessive accumulation of debt, as investors borrow money to buy into the boom. Historically, many asset bubbles go hand in hand with the creation of new forms of credit or debt that afford investors new opportunities to participate in speculative trading.

Basel III This is a new capital adequacy standard developed by global banking regulators in the wake of the great financial crash that effectively triples the size of the capital reserves that the world's banks must hold against losses. Basel III sets a new key capital (adequacy) ratio of 4.5 per cent of assets, plus a new buffer of a further 2.5 per cent. Introduced in 2010 under the auspices of the Bank for International Settlements based in Basel, Switzerland, the new rules are being phased in from January 2013 through to January 2019 (see ft.com/lexicon).

Bond A bond is a form of loan that can be easily traded and sold. Instead of companies or governments raising money to finance long-term investments (or, in the case of governments, to finance current expenditure) by securing a loan from a commercial bank(s), they sell bonds to investors, initially by issuing them to a financial market known as the primary bond market. Once purchased from the primary bond market, corporate and government bonds can then be bought and sold on the secondary bond market. The holder of the bond is the lender (creditor), the issuer of the bond is the borrower (debtor), and the coupon is the interest payable to the lender by the issuer (Wikipedia).

The investor – often a large domestic or foreign bank, a pension fund, a hedge fund, an insurance company or a sovereign wealth fund that manages the money of royal families or governments with large oil revenues – is lending money to a company or government in return for a promise to repay the loan on a specified date in the future, at a fixed rate of interest. Government (sovereign) bonds are usually viewed as the safest form of investment because governments have access to tax income as a means to guarantee repayment. But if the bond markets become concerned that a government might not be able to meet its bond repayments, the price that its existing bonds will trade at on the secondary market will be reduced. This affects the bonds' 'yield'.

For example, the price of 10-year Greek government bonds issued in March 2010 with an original value of €1,000, and paying an interest rate of 6.25 per cent, had fallen to €420 in August 2011, as that was the most that anyone would pay for them in the secondary market. Since existing bonds were being bought and sold at lower prices than their nominal value, but the interest remained constant, so the bonds' yield had increased to nearly 15 per cent. But just as the yield on existing bonds increased, so, too, did the interest rate (coupon) demanded by investors on new Greek bond issues, making it much more expensive for Greece to renew or refinance its current level of debt (Laskaridis, 2014, p 26).

Capital At its most simple, a firm's capital is the difference between the value of its assets and the value of its liabilities. Total capital includes the company's debt, as raised from its creditors, and its shareholders' equity (see 'stocks, shares and equity'). In the particular language of banking regulation, capital is the amount of 'unborrowed', as opposed to borrowed, money that a bank uses to make its loans and other investments.

Collateralised debt obligations (CDOs) These pool together cash flow-generating assets and repackage them into discrete tranches offering different combinations of risk and return that can be sold on to investors (Coggan, 2009, p 194). The pooled assets, such as mortgages, government and corporate bonds, and consumer debt such as car loans, are essentially debt obligations that serve as collateral for the CDO. In theory, CDOs attract a stronger credit rating than individual assets due to the risk being more diversified (see also 'securitisation').

Prior to the credit crunch, investment banks sold CDOs to investors for three reasons:

- the funds they received gave the banks more cash to make new loans;
- their sale moved the loan's risk of defaulting from the bank to the investors;
- CDOs gave banks a new and more profitable product to sell, which boosted their share prices and their managers and traders' bonuses.

One knowledgeable insider has described CDOs as 'casino operations masquerading as innovation' (Smith, 2011, p 297). They remained a niche product until 2003-04, when the US housing boom led the investment banks involved in issuing CDOs to turn their attention to non-prime mortgage-backed securities (MBS) as a new source of collateral for them. CDOs subsequently exploded in popularity, with the three biggest rating agencies (Fitch, Moody's and Standard & Poor's) (agencies whose income derives from fees paid by the investment banks and other institutions which issue the products they are rating) giving many of them AAA ratings, and CDO sales rising almost 10-fold from 2003 to 2006 (Investopedia).

Conduits and special purpose vehicles (SPVs) These constitute a network of 'off-balance sheet' vehicles set up by commercial banks as separate legal entities to hold residential mortgages and other assets such as car loans and credit card debt. In the 1990s these pools of assets were assembled into vast numbers of 'securitised' investment products, and conduits and SPVs were created in order to move the assets off the sponsoring bank's balance sheet, where they would be forced by capital adequacy regulations to restrict their overall amount of lending. Conduits and SPVs are registered in tax havens or 'secrecy jurisdictions', and form part of the shadow banking system.

Mention should be made here, perhaps, of the 'dodgiest' members of the conduit family, the structured investment vehicles or SIVs, which had no formal support from their sponsoring bank, the lowest quality of assets (often sub-prime mortgage bonds) and the highest levels of borrowing. Once they went bust in the great financial crash, however, investors demanded that their sponsors intervene, often crippling the parent bank (Smith, 2011, p 239).

Credit This is the ability to purchase something without immediately paying for it, through a credit card, a bank loan, a mortgage or some other form of credit. The creation of credit is the most important source of new money, and new spending power, in the economy. Of course, once obtained, credit is immediately converted into debt to be repaid, with interest, over a given period of time.

The great financial crash of 2008 came at the end of a long period during which financial activity and credit creation by international banks grew markedly more rapidly than the growth rate of real economies. Light-touch regulation allowed the financial sector to offer a wider range of products to a wider range of customers, but it is clear that a large proportion of this increased credit was related to the property market (both residential and commercial), and that its main impact was to increase asset prices rather than add to the productive potential of non-financial firms.

Credit and debt are more than just financial categories. Personal and national indebtedness has long been bound up with strong emotions of shame, guilt and powerlessness, while creditors have been extolled as virtuous and prudent, and credit worthiness regarded as the embodiment of moral worth. Although the rise of consumerism and the availability of easy credit have reshaped traditional attitudes, moral ambiguity about these categories remains commonplace (Dyson, 2015).

Credit default swaps (CDS) A CDS, a type of derivative, is basically an insurance policy that provides protection to the purchaser of a mortgage-backed security (MBS), collateralised debt obligation (CDO), other asset-backed security or corporate or government bond. It is called a 'swap' rather than an insurance policy because an insurance policy requires reserves to be set aside to pay out claims against the policy, whereas swaps do not. Banks and other financial institutions such as hedge funds typically buy CDS.

Many institutions that invested in MBS in the housing boom leading up to the great financial crash entered into CDS contracts to protect against default. Such institutions make a series of payments (the CDS fee or 'spread') to the protection seller over the life of the contract (typically five years) in exchange for a guarantee that they will be compensated if the loan defaults. For example, a bank that has made a loan to a country such as Greece with a sovereign debt problem may choose to 'hedge' the loan by buying CDS protection on Greece. The bank makes periodic payments to the CDS seller. If Greece defaults on its sovereign debt repayments, the CDS seller is obliged to buy the loans from the bank at their full face value.

Facilitated by technical innovation, the volume of this kind of financial activity grew significantly after 2003, reaching US$58 trillion by 2008 (Mason, 2009, p 189). CDS contracts are not just used for hedging; investors use them to speculate on whether a borrower such as Greece will default. Credit default swaps can be freely traded, and can be struck even if the buyer does not own the debt they wish to insure. This creates a problem of *moral hazard*: such a buyer benefits if there is a default and therefore has an incentive to take actions that may encourage default.

The market for such swaps dried up amid the financial crisis, and has yet to return to previous levels. As MBS and CDOs became nearly worthless, the banks and hedge funds selling CDS found themselves having to pay out big money. Most banks and hedge funds, however, were simultaneously on both sides of the CDS trade. They would buy CDS protection on the one hand, and then sell CDS protection to someone else at the same time. When a bond defaulted, the banks might have to pay some money out, but they'd also be getting money back in. They 'netted out', in the jargon.

Everyone, that is, except for AIG (American International Group). Banks all over the world bought CDS protection from AIG, but AIG was on one side of these trades only: they aggressively sold CDS in the belief that they would only have to pay out very few, if any, of the swaps. They never bought. Credit default swaps written by AIG covered more than US$440 billion in bonds (Davidson, 2008), but once bonds started defaulting, AIG had to pay out and nobody was paying AIG. The resulting liquidity crisis bankrupted AIG, prompting the Federal Reserve (the Fed) (the US central bank) to extend a US$85 billion line of credit. The lack of visibility into the CDS positions of different institutions and how they might or might not 'net out' against one another more than anything else earned CDS their classification as 'financial weapons of mass destruction'.

Credit derivatives These are financial assets like forward contracts, swaps and options (see 'derivatives') whose price is driven by the credit or default risk of a corporate or government borrower, and which allow that risk to be transferred to a third party. For example, a bank concerned that one of its customers may not be able to repay a loan can protect itself against loss by transferring the credit risk to another party while keeping the loan on its books (Investopedia).

Derivatives Broadly defined, these are contracts that allow banks to trade financial assets whose resale value depends on ('derives' from) the value of an underlying asset or benchmark which is subject to change over time – such as commodities, bonds, equities, currencies or interest rates – and is therefore difficult to predict (Tett, 2009, p 322). A derivative is effectively a bet that pays out based on how a particular asset, rate or index performs over a particular time period.

The four main types of derivatives contracts are: forwards, futures, options and swaps. Forwards and futures contracts are agreements to complete a financial transaction at a specified price and quantity at a future (forward) date. Futures are traded on organised exchanges via a clearinghouse, which minimises risk to the parties (and the clearinghouse) because collateral is required from both sides. Forwards, unlike futures, are customised through negotiation and traded over the counter (OTC). They are executed privately, in most cases through commercial and investment banks that either find a counter-party for the other side of the contract or serve as the counter-party themselves. Since such contracts are bilateral, the participants are exposed to counter-party risk, meaning that no third party stands between them to guarantee performance of the contract.

An option gives you the right, but not the obligation, to buy or sell something at a specified future date for a specified price. Futures are the same as options except that they bring with them the obligation to buy or sell at the specified price; with futures, you are committed to the deal. It follows that futures are much riskier than options (Lanchester, 2008). A swap is a contract to exchange a set of payments one party owns for a set of payments owned by the other. The type most commonly traded is the interest rate swap, which has increased in importance as financial institutions seek to manage interest rate risk. Swaps, like forwards, are traded on the OTC market and are subject to counter-party risk.

Derivatives allow investors and banks to protect against risk by hedging. Thus, farmers facing an uncertain harvest are very grateful for the opportunity to sell their next season's produce at a fixed price, guaranteed in advance. The first formal commodities exchange, the Chicago Board of Trade, was established in 1848 to provide a centralised location for negotiating forward contracts. Under its aegis, the first exchange-traded derivatives contracts were listed in 1865, and in 1925 the first futures clearinghouse was formed (Prahba et al, 2014). Because they are bought not for the full cost of the underlying asset, but for the advance premium, with the balance being borrowed from a bank or broker (an individual or firm in the business of buying and selling securities), they offer a cheap and flexible form of insurance against things going wrong.

But derivatives can also be used to take on more risk and increase the level of reward. In particular, the technique of 'tranching' mortgage-backed securities enabled the banks to pay the holders of the different tranches different interest rates according to how risky a tranche they bought. This ability to appeal to both investors who wanted low risk and modest returns and investors with a greater risk appetite and a desire for greater returns led to an explosion of demand for mortgage-backed securities as US house prices nearly doubled between 1997 and 2006. Mortgage-backed securities were no longer a simple equity hedge, but objects of speculative investment in their own right (Blyth, 2013, pp 27-30). Investors 'levered up' their exposure to the market by using money borrowed from the banks to purchase additional securities.

Derivatives activity is highly concentrated. In the US banking system, over 90 per cent of derivative instruments are held by just four large, complex financial institutions (LCFIs): JP Morgan Chase, Citigroup, Bank of America and Goldman Sachs (Prabha et al, 2014). Close links have developed between these banks, hedge funds and oil companies: the British sociologist John Urry reports that futures traders such as banks and hedge funds, with no intention of taking physical delivery of energy but only of turning a paper profit, today control 80 per cent of the energy futures markets (Urry, 2014, pp 113-4).

Fannie Mae and Freddie Mac These are nicknames for the Federal National Mortgage Association (FNMA) and Federal Home Loan Mortgage Corporation (FHLMC) respectively, government-sponsored enterprises providing financing for the US residential mortgage market. Fannie Mae was created by the US government as a federal agency in 1938 in the Great Depression era, to make mortgages more easily available to low-income families. Basically, it guaranteed the mortgages originated by other lenders, so reducing the risk if borrowers defaulted on their loan (Lowe, 2011, p 170). In 1968 it was converted into a private corporation with a congressional charter. Freddie Mac was created in 1970 to provide support for the secondary mortgage market, again as a private corporation with a congressional charter (Thompson, 2009, p 17). Both were mandated to meet 'affordable housing' policy goals, by allocating a specified part of their mortgage business to serve low- and moderate-income borrowers. They also bought and held enormous portfolios of mortgage-backed securities (MBS) for investment purposes (Ferguson, 2014, pp 75-6). Between them, they became the channel through which a large part of the secondary mortgage market operated.

The MBS issued by Fannie Mae and Freddie Mac were particularly attractive to investors because, although government officials repeatedly denied that their bonds were guaranteed by the US federal government, there was a widespread perception to the contrary in the markets. This allowed Fannie Mae and Freddie Mac to borrow at below market rates while central banks became willing to buy their debt in the same way as US Treasury bonds to hold as foreign exchange reserves (Thompson, 2009, p 17).

Financial Stability Board (FSB) The FSB is an international panel of central bankers, finance officials and regulators established at the G20 summit in London in 2009 to monitor and make recommendations about the global financial system. The G20 or Group of Twenty is a forum bringing together the governments and central bank governors from 20 major economies. At a meeting of its finance ministers in Sydney in February 2014, the G20 agreed to adopt a common tax reporting standard to combat transfer pricing (transnational corporations unjustifiably shifting taxable profits from one country to another). See also 'regulatory arbitrage'.

Financialisation Perhaps the most useful way to think about financialisation is as a term to describe processes in which ownability, investability and tradeability are extended. Something becomes financialised by becoming ownable, followed by becoming more widely investable via financial instruments, which in turn become widely tradeable (Scott, 2013, p 24).

Academics use the term to denote the trend whereby the financial system and financial activity including various forms of lending and securitisation are increasing in scale and significance, and the related tendency for profit-making in the economy to occur increasingly through financial channels rather than through productive activities in the real economy (Krippner, 2012, p 4). The figures are truly astonishing. In 2007, on the eve of the great financial crash, the total value of derivate instruments stood at US$596 trillion – eight times the size of the real economy – and the total amount of currency traded amounted to US$1,168 trillion, or 17 times world GDP (Mason, 2009, p 66, citing statistics compiled by the Bank for International Settlements and the World Bank, a bank that provides loans to developing countries and to the 'transition economies' of Eastern and South East Europe).

This trend is not confined to the financial sector and financial sector profits: non-financial firms, too, have become increasingly dependent on financial revenues as a supplement to earnings from traditional productive activities (Krippner, 2012, p 3).

More broadly, financialisation refers to the process whereby financial markets, financial institutions and financial elites gain an increasing hold over state policies and economic outcomes in mature capitalist democracies. This is particularly the case in the US and the UK, with their reliance in the boom years preceding the credit crunch on a model of economic growth based on excessive consumer debt secured against rising property prices. Financialisation in this sense is intimately linked to the growth of the shadow banking system and to what might be termed the toxic combination of unfettered financial markets and unfettered executive pay (see Chapter Four).

For some commentators, finance, in the current era, is at the core of a new social settlement in which the fabric of Western society and Western economies has been reworked. Not only do we now rely less on the manufacture of things and more on the manufacture of credit, but finance and financialisation also mould our economy, geography, ideology and politics. 'Finance thinking' gets inside our heads and has become society's 'common sense', removing the dominant economic growth orthodoxy from political contestation (Massey, 2013).

The related notion of the 'financialisation of everyday life' (Lowe, 2011, p 199) refers to a process whereby new mortgage products have become the channel for global financial institutions to reach down to people's homes and domestic budgets, encouraging homeowners to unlock the equity in their major financial asset. The process of remortgaging (taking on more mortgage debt and releasing capital to spend immediately) has, in turn, reshaped the contemporary welfare state because it has enabled homeowners to service their welfare needs, as well as their consumption wants, through the private market, and so break the circle of reliance on the state.

Financial repression This is a term used to describe measures sometimes used by governments to boost their coffers and/or reduce their debt. These measures include the deliberate attempt to hold down interest rates to below inflation, making it cheaper for the government to continue borrowing at the expense of hard-done-by savers (see lexicon.ft.com). Financial repression can be considered a form of taxation in the sense that 'unlike income, consumption, or sales taxes, the "repression" tax rate (or rates) are determined by financial regulations ... that are opaque.... Given that deficit reduction usually involves highly unpopular expenditure reductions and (or) tax increases ... the relatively "stealthier" financial repression tax may be a more politically palatable alternative to authorities faced with the need to reduce outstanding debts' (Reinhart and Sbrancia, 2011, p 19).

Foreclosure This refers to a situation in which a homeowner is unable to make full payments on his or her mortgage, which allows the lender to seize the property, evict the homeowner and sell the home, as stipulated in the mortgage contract (Investopedia).

Glass-Steagall and its repeal The Glass-Steagall Act 1933, enacted by the US Congress during the Great Depression, prevented commercial banks from trading securities with their clients' deposits. Glass-Steagall was eventually repealed during the Clinton administration by the Gramm-Leach-Bliley Act 1999. The term Glass-Steagall usually refers to the set of rules that kept a commercial bank from engaging in speculative, risky trading with customers' deposits. If a bank took deposits, it could not trade in anything other than government bonds; if it underwrote securities or facilitated their trading, it could not take deposits.

Glass-Steagall is one of the series of 'New Deal' domestic policy reforms introduced in the US between 1933 and 1938 (plus a few that came later) in response to the Great Depression. With the arrival of the New Deal, the federal government took on a much more active role in redistributing income through the tax code and public programmes, in constructing a new industrial relations system, in regulating corporations and the financial system, and in making big investments in public education and research (Hacker and Pierson, 2011, p 55-6).

US economist Joseph Stiglitz, among many others, argues that Gramm-Leach-Bliley – the culmination of a sustained lobbying effort by the banking and financial services industries to reduce regulation in their sector – contributed to the 2008 financial crash by ensuring that when investment and commercial banks were brought together again, it was the investment bank culture that came out on top (Stiglitz, 2010, pp 162-3).

Hedge fund A hedge fund is a private, largely unregulated investment fund which uses a range of sophisticated strategies to maximise returns. Hedge fund managers make their money through fees; investors make their money from the high-risk investments they authorise the manager to make. Many hedge funds grew out of the proprietary trading activity of investment banks in the 1980s and 1990s. It is not without irony that US sub-prime mortgages – loans to poor people – were sold as securities and bought in substantial numbers by hedge funds – financial institutions that typically serve the rich (Stockhammer, 2014).

As their name implies, hedge funds often seek to offset potential losses by hedging their investments using a variety of methods, so that they stand to profit whatever the outcome of a deal. However, the term 'hedge fund' has come in modern parlance to be applied to many funds that use 'hedging' methods to increase risk, and therefore financial return, rather than to reduce it. The assets managed by a hedge fund can run into many billions of dollars, and their sway over financial markets is considerable (see Augar, 2010, chapter 4).

International Monetary Fund (IMF) The IMF is an organisation of 188 member countries set up towards the end of the Second World War to promote international monetary cooperation and exchange rate stability. It provides loans to member countries having difficulty meeting their international payments, and to assist with poverty reduction, generally on the condition that those countries implement 'free market' policies and programmes (otherwise known as 'structural adjustment policies'). These typically consist of a package of measures that include currency devaluation, liberalisation and deregulation of trade and investment, privatisation of state-owned enterprises and cuts in public spending to reduce budget deficits.

Mark to market accounting This requires banks to accept as true values of their loans and mortgages the prices set by the financial markets for these assets. Problems can arise when the market-based measurement does not accurately reflect the underlying asset's true value. This can occur when a company is forced to calculate the selling price of assets or liabilities during unfavourable or volatile times, such as a financial crisis or liquidity crunch, when the market price of an asset is likely to be much lower than the underlying value.

Similarly, mark to market accounting created a mirage of rapidly rising asset values during the 'boom' years preceding the crash, allowing banks to report illusory profits and creating a large demand for more debt issuance through securitisation (see http://shadowbanking. weebly.com/mark-to-market-leverage.html).

Monetary policy This refers to the policies of the central bank. During the years of the Great Moderation, central banks came to focus almost exclusively on controlling the short-term interest rate, usually through an inflation-targeting regime (Davies, 2015, p 28). For example, by changing the Bank Rate – the rate of interest that the Bank of England pays on reserve balances held by commercial banks – the Bank of England is able to influence a range of other borrowing and lending rates set by financial institutions, and hence the general level of spending in the economy. But monetary policy can also be used to support other objectives. The US Federal Reserve's (Fed's) current statutory mandate, for example, calls for it to 'promote effectively the goals of maximum employment, stable prices, and moderate long-term interest rates'.

A central bank can also issue fiat money: paper currency made legal tender by government fiat. This allows it to engage in unorthodox policies such as printing money to buy up government debts and other assets (see 'quantitative easing'). A central bank can also tighten capital adequacy rules on banks, thereby constraining credit creation. Since the financial crash, central banks have lowered interest rates to historic lows in an effort to stimulate investment and consumer spending – at the time of writing (October 2015), rates are 0.25 per cent in the US, 0.50 per cent in the UK and 0.05 per cent in the Eurozone.

Money markets Also known as wholesale markets, the money markets are the global network of dealers and investors who issue and buy and sell *short-term* debt securities. Money markets should be distinguished from the capital markets, in which corporate equity and longer-term debt securities, including government bonds, are issued and traded.

The money markets are used by big corporations and by governments to obtain funds to manage their short-term cash needs without having to issue shares or bonds. This is done by trading interest-bearing securities with high 'liquidity' (meaning that they are easily convertible into cash) and short maturities. Money market financial instruments are generally considered very safe investments that return a relatively low interest rate in exchange for temporary cash storage over a short period (Luttrell et al, 2012). In the US, federal, state and local governments all issue 'paper' to meet funding needs. States and local governments issue municipal paper, while the US Treasury issues Treasury bills to fund the US public debt (see 'sovereign debt').

The bulk of trading in the money markets consists of inter-bank lending that is often benchmarked to the London Interbank Offered Rate (LIBOR) for the appropriate currency and maturity (from overnight to 12 months). The freezing-up of the inter-bank wholesale lending market in late 2007 effectively transformed what was a credit or liquidity crunch into a full-blown financial crisis. This is because the inter-bank market had become increasingly central to the operation of the global payments system. With seven out of every ten transactions taking place in US dollars, it was the most important focus of the Federal Reserve's (Fed's) monetary policy, with a select few Wall Street banks, operating as 'market makers', reallocating the liquidity provided by the Fed.

The increasing spread between the federal funds rate (the interest rate at which US banks borrow funds maintained at the Fed from each other on an overnight basis) and LIBOR (the interest rate that banks charge each other on the London money market for short-term loans), as banks feared that their loans to other banks might not be repaid, endangered the Fed's capacity to manage the global financial system, obliging it to provide access to adequate amounts of dollar holdings to banks all over the world to enable them to meet their obligations (Panitch and Gindin, 2013, pp 312-3).

Money market funds (MMFs) In the US, a money market fund (MMF) (also known as a money market mutual fund) is a type of low-risk, low-return mutual fund that raises money from individual savers and invests that money in short-term debt securities issued by the federal government or blue-chip companies. MMF managers aim to keep the value of the initial investment constant (MMF shares always being worth US$1), so investors do not benefit from a rise in the value of their capital, but from interest and dividend payments. First established in 1971, MMFs became attractive to millions of middle-class Americans as a seemingly low-risk alternative to bank savings accounts, but one offering a better rate of interest (Mason, 2009, p 191).

Investors placing their cash in MMFs assume that they can withdraw it at short notice, and for this reason MMFs usually only want to purchase assets that have a short duration and are safe, such as commercial paper (CP) (see 'asset-backed commercial paper') and US Treasury bills (Tett, 2009, pp 205-7). MMFs became increasingly important to the wholesale money market in the period leading up to the credit crunch. In a chain reaction, anxieties about the bursting of the housing bubble led investors to withdraw their money from MMFs, and MMFs to stop lending to the banks.

The collapse of Lehman Brothers in September 2008 precipitated a 'silent run' (through withdrawal of money from internet accounts) on a MMF sector by this time worth US$4 trillion, causing some money market funds to 'break the buck', meaning that a dollar invested in them was no longer worth a dollar. To avoid a meltdown, the US federal government was forced to provide a blanket guarantee to all existing MMFs (Roubini and Mihm, 2011, p 35).

Monoline insurers These are a class of insurance companies whose single line of business is to insure securities and bonds. Corporations and public institutions such as municipalities issue bonds to raise funds for, say, a new factory or a new school or hospital. Monoline insurance companies were set up in the 1970s to insure against the risk that such bonds would default. Paying a fee to a 'monoline' to insure the debt (to guarantee repayment of principal and interest in the event of default) helps to raise the credit rating of government or corporate bonds, which in turn means the issuer can raise the money more cheaply. Along with AIG (American International Group), monoline insurers suffered heavy losses in the credit crunch as a result of insuring securities backed by sub-prime mortgages.

Mortgage-backed securities (**MBS**) These are bonds whose value is secured, or backed, by the value of an underlying bundle of mortgages. When you buy a MBS, you are not buying the actual mortgage. Instead, you are buying a promise to be paid the return or cash flow of mortgage payments that the bundle will receive. The MBS is a 'derivative' security, because its value is derived from the underlying asset.

Investors buying MBS receive income when the original house buyers make their mortgage payments, but they also inherit the risk that interest rates may rise and thereby precipitate a wave of mortgage defaults. The quality of MBS, in other words, depends very much on their original source. In the event, the scale of debt built up in the sub-prime mortgage market in the US during the boom years was enormous, and since so many pension funds and financial institutions owned MBS, they all took heavy losses when the housing bubble burst in the summer of 2007.

Mutual fund A mutual fund, also known as a unit trust in the UK, is a financial institution that pools money from many different investors to purchase and professionally manage a portfolio of stocks (equities), bonds and other assets.

Pension fund A pension fund is a professionally managed investment fund established by an employer from which retirement income is paid, accumulated from contributions from the employer and employees.

Private equity This is finance provided in return for an equity stake in potentially high growth companies. However, instead of going to the stock market and selling shares to raise capital, private equity firms raise funds from institutional investors such as pension funds, insurance companies, endowments and high net worth individuals (see www. bvca.co.uk/PrivateEquityExplained/FAQsinPrivateEquity.aspx).

Private equity firms use this equity funding, augmented by large amounts of borrowed money, to buy majority control of under-performing or under-valued companies, reorganise them, and then sell them on at a profit when the business goes public (that is, when its shares are floated on the stock exchange). This investment strategy is known as the 'leveraged buy-out' (LBO). It involves private equity investors loading debt onto the balance sheets of firms, which then have little choice but to sell off assets and squeeze the wages of their workers (Stockhammer, 2014).

Football (soccer) fans, particularly supporters of Manchester United Football Club (MUFC), may already be familiar with the LBO. MUFC, then a public company with shareholders and free of debt, was sold in 2005 to the Glazer brothers, a US private equity company, in a LBO, saddling the club with a debt of £525 million secured against its assets. For a number of years, investment in players had to take second place to maximising the amount paid out to the club's creditors (Sayer, 2015, pp 212-3).

Quantitative easing (QE) Usually, central banks try to raise the amount of lending and activity in the economy indirectly, by cutting interest rates. Lower interest rates encourage people to spend, not save. But when interest rates can go no lower, a central bank's only option is to pump money into the economy directly. This is quantitative easing (QE). In the UK, the Bank of England began its programme of 'asset purchases' in January 2009. As of March 2013, the Bank had committed a total of £375 billion to QE.

Central banks increase the supply of money by 'printing' more of it. In the UK, the Bank of England has used this new money to buy up government bonds (gilts) from banks and other financial institutions.

In return, the banks receive new money (deposits) that has come into existence through QE. Theoretically, when the economy has recovered, the Bank sells the bonds it has bought and destroys the cash it receives. That means that in the long term there has been no extra cash created.

Regulatory arbitrage This is the practice whereby financial institutions and transnational corporations capitalise on loopholes in regulatory systems in order to circumvent unfavourable regulation. Prior to the financial crash, bankers who wanted more freedom to take risks practised regulatory arbitrage by increasingly shifting banking activities to the shadow banks. So, too, transnational corporations making a product in one country for sale in another can transfer it first, to an affiliate in that second country, which then sells it to the customer. The price at which the transfer occurs can be manipulated to ensure that greater profits arise in the country with the lower tax rate (Brooks, 2013, p 125).

Repurchase agreements (repos) In a repo agreement, one party sells an asset (usually fixed-income securities such as government or corporate bonds) to another party in exchange for cash, and commits to repurchase the asset at a higher price within a short period, often the next day. If the seller defaults during the life of the repo, the buyer can sell the asset to a third party to offset the loss (see www.icmagroup.org).

Securitisation The 'securitisation' process is a means of creating a market for the buying and selling of illiquid assets such as residential mortgages or credit card or car loans. Instead of existing solely as a promise by a home buyer to pay back the money, a mortgage became a piece of paper that could itself be sold and re-sold for speculative profit on financial markets (Stanford, 2008).

'Securitisation takes place when an originator, a bank or another type of lender (like an auto company that also provides car loans or leases), sells its loans ("assets", since they generate income) to a special purpose vehicle' (Smith, 2011, p 236). A pool of such illiquid assets is converted into tradeable securities by being 'sliced and diced' into portions and sold on to third parties in tranches, each with a different combination of risk and reward, rather than being retained on the bank's balance sheet. Risk is thereby transferred to the third party, and the bank is able to raise funds to finance new lending.

Securitisation most commonly involves taking the debt from a number of mortgages and combining them to make mortgage-backed securities (MBS), which can then be traded on the open market. In theory this is a 'secure' form of investment because by buying bundles of mortgages, investors are reducing their exposure to the risk of individual loans defaulting – the end buyer holds a very small slice of a very large number of supposedly 'uncorrelated' mortgage loans.

Originally, securitisation was limited to pools of assets that had explicit or implicit guarantees from the US government, but during the housing boom the home loans underlying these securities were mostly sourced through a new breed of largely unregulated mortgage lenders that obtained their funding from Wall Street investment banks and existed only to feed the securitisation 'food chain' (Ferguson, 2014, p 60). The end result was to transform securitisation from a specialist technique used mainly by US banks and mortgage guarantee institutions into a global banking phenomenon (Augar, 2010, p 12).

Security A security is a tradeable financial asset of any kind such as a share or a government, corporate or mortgage bond (see 'mortgage-backed securities'). Separately, the term 'security' is also used to mean something that is pledged as collateral by a borrower when taking out a loan. For example, mortgages in the UK are usually secured on the value of the borrower's property that is gradually being paid off or 'amortised' over a period of 20 to 25 years. This means that if the borrower cannot repay, the lender can repossess the security (the house) and sell it in order to help repay the outstanding debt.

Short selling This is a technique used by investors who think the price of an asset such as shares or a commodity will fall. They borrow the asset from another investor and then sell it on in the relevant market.

The aim is to buy back the asset at a lower price and return it to its owner, pocketing the difference. This is also known as 'shorting'.

Sovereign debt Also known as 'government debt' or the 'national debt', sovereign debt is often issued as bonds denominated in a reserve currency (a strong currency widely used in international trade that a central bank is prepared to hold as part of its foreign exchange reserves, typically the US dollar). The less likely it is that the financial markets think the bond will be repaid, the higher the 'yield' the government will be forced to pay bondholders – and the higher the cost of servicing the sovereign debt.

Stocks, shares and equity These are all words used to describe essentially the same thing. The stock of a company is partitioned into shares. When you buy a company's shares you are buying ownership of part of the company and you become a shareholder – you are investing your money in the company by buying an 'equity' stake which is rewarded by the payment of dividends. Shares in companies are bought and sold on stock markets such as the New York, London or Tokyo stock exchanges.

Structured finance The essential feature of structured finance is the practice of bundling bonds or other loans into complex investment products where the investor can choose the risks on offer, as assessed by a credit rating agency. For a rather more colourful description of how structured finance worked in the boom years preceding the crash, which is particularly scathing about the part played by the credit rating agencies in the process, see Mason (2009, pp 91-5).

Tail risk A well-managed financial firm takes calculated and limited risks, so why did the banks not see the financial crash coming? Basically, because they under-estimated tail risk – risks that occur very rarely because they happen in the tail of a probability distribution. The banks' 'value at risk' models of the future assumed a normally distributed replication of the past, so blinding them to the possibility of a high-impact, non-normal event taking place in the tail of a distribution, in this case, the chance that much higher than anticipated mortgage default correlations across the US would lead to all the banks' mortgage-backed assets losing value at the same time.

Why did the banks take on tail risk in the first place? The answer lies in the incentives that are present within a deregulated, competitive financial system to 'out-perform the market'. Raghuram Rajan makes the point succinctly:

At times when financing is plentiful, so that there is intense competition among bankers and fund managers, the need to create alpha (excess returns) pushes many of them inexorably toward taking on tail risk....Because these incentives are present throughout the financial firm, there is little reason to expect that top management will curb the practice. Indeed, the checks and balances at each level of the corporate hierarchy broke down.... A seemingly irrational frenzy may be a product of all-too-rational calculations by financial firms. (Rajan, 2010, p 139)

Index

Note: **app** refers to the appendix.